Difficult Gospel

Difficult Gospel

The Theology of Rowan Williams

Mike Higton

CHURCH PUBLISHING
New York

A catalog record for this book is available from the
Library of Congress

ISBN 0-89869-470-1

Church Publishing Incorporated
445 Fifth Avenue
New York, NY 10016

Contents

Acknowledgements

I have many people to thank for their guidance, assistance and companionship. There is my teacher, colleague and friend David Ford who first suggested that I write this book; there is Anna Hardman who commissioned it for SCM Press, and Barbara Laing who did not push me too hard when it first came to the deadline. There are many who helped me find more of Williams' texts, or pointed out to me discussions of Williams in the media – Julian Nangle of Julian Nangle Rare Books in Dorchester, William Richardson and Oliver Creighton in the University of Exeter, Alan Murray, the Churches' National Adviser in Further Education, June Evans, the administrator of the Bevan Foundation, and Paul Butler of the Jubilee Group. There are those friends and relatives who tried to make me write less like a constipated academic, and more like someone who had met ordinary English: my wife Hester, my mother Patricia, and my friend Chris Goringe; there are Jane and Jonathan Gledhill, who generously put me up during some lectures Williams gave in Salisbury; there are all my colleagues in the Departments of Theology and Lifelong Learning in Exeter, who allowed me to have enough study leave to write; and, of course, there is Rowan Williams himself, who made time to talk to me about the project, and who was kind enough to check the typescript for my more laughable errors. I am very grateful to all of these. The book is dedicated, however, to someone whose longed-for arrival wonderfully interrupted, delayed, and disrupted the whole thing: my beautiful daughter Bridget, who I imagine will be totally uninterested in it unless an edition is published with a strokeable beard on the front, or a squeak concealed in the final pages (I've done my best) – or unless it is delivered to our house in nice scrunchy packaging. However, because it will forever be associated in my mind with the first exhilarating, shattering, bewildering and joyful weeks of her life, this book is dedicated to her.

Abbreviations

A	*Arius: Heresy and Tradition* (London: SCM Press, 2001; 1st edn 1987)
COT	*Christ on Trial* (Grand Rapids: Zondervan, 2002)
DL	*The Dwelling of the Light* (Norwich: Canterbury Press, 2003)
LI	*Lost Icons* (Edinburgh: T&T Clark, 2000)
LRW	*Love's Redeeming Work* (Oxford: OUP, 2001)
OCT	*On Christian Theology* (Oxford: Blackwell, 2000)
OTJ	*Open to Judgement* (London: DLT, 2002; 1st edn 1994)
PTT	*Ponder These Things* (Norwich: Canterbury Press, 2002)
R	*Resurrection* (London: DLT, 2002; 1st edn: 1982)
TA	*Teresa of Avila* (London: Continuum, 2000; 1st edn 1991)
TG	*The Truce of God* (London: Collins/Fount, 1983)
TVNL	*The Theology of Vladimir Nikolaievich Lossky: An Exposition and Critique* (Williams' doctoral thesis, University of Oxford, 1975)
WK	*The Wound of Knowledge* (London: DLT, 2002; 1st edn 1979)

Introduction

Difficult Gospel

I

Last month, I found myself sitting in an airport departure lounge littered with people in transit: people from more backgrounds than I could guess, speakers of more languages than I was able to recognize, all accidentally thrown together in a cluttered public space in which few of us ever spoke more than a handful of words to any of those around us. I was on my way to what was for me an important meeting, finishing some university business I had been negotiating for months; I was nervous, defensive, concerned to make a good impression when I arrived at my destination. With some dull time to fill before my flight was called, I tried to decide how to begin this description of Rowan Williams' theology. In particular, I tried to think of a way to convey the claim that in the two or more million words of his published writings he is constantly concerned to press one simple question – and I realized that I could not think about that question without asking how it caught up with me exactly there, exactly then.

Sitting there, I was aware of the work-stale glances of the airport staff, of the quickly averted eyes of my fellow travellers, of the anticipated scrutiny of those I was going to meet, of the assessing gaze of my employers carried around in my head, and of my own anxious self-regard. What difference would it have made if I had let myself believe that, beyond all these, I was held in a wholly loving gaze? What difference would it have made if I believed myself subject to a gaze which saw all my surface accidents and arrangements, all my inner habits and inheritances, all my anxieties and arrogances, all my history – and yet a gaze which nevertheless loved that whole tangled bundle which makes me the self I am, with an utterly free, utterly selfless love? What difference would it have made if I let myself believe that I was held in a loving gaze that saw all the twists and distortions of my messy self, all the harm that it can do and has done, but also saw all that it could become, all that it could give to others, and all that it could receive?

And what difference would it have made if I had seen each face around me in that departure lounge – cleaners, businessmen, emigrants and immigrants, waitresses, tourists, even academics on university business – as individually held in the same over-whelming, loving gaze? What difference would it have made if I believed each person around me to be loved with the same focus, by a love which saw each person's unique history, unique problems, unique capacity, unique gift? And what difference would it have made if I believed that this love nevertheless made no distinctions between people more worthy and people less worthy of love, no distinctions of race, religion, age, innocence, strength, or beauty: a lavish and indiscriminate love?

It was easy to jot these simple questions down, easy to think *about* them – but to *believe* in such a loving regard, and to let belief in it percolate down through all the sedimented layers of my awareness, would have been shattering. Such unfettered acceptance would have been utterly disarming; to believe such good news, such a Gospel, would have been very, very difficult.

II

It is this difficulty, the difficulty of the Gospel, which is the most interesting difficulty in Rowan Williams' writings. There are, of course, other kinds of difficulty. When his appointment as the 104th Archbishop of Canterbury was announced, most of the profiles and interviews and assessments and editorials which spread like dandelions across the international press mentioned that he was a prolific theological author – but many quickly excused themselves from giving any account of his writings by explaining that what he had written was 'formidable', 'complex', 'dense' – and 'difficult'. What they had in mind, of course, was not the searching, disarranging, devastating difficulty of the Gospel, but the more ordinary difficulty of academic jargon, involved argument, abstruse references and subtle distinctions. I feel considerable sympathy for this assessment, having spent much of the past year reading or re-reading Williams' seventeen books (not to mention the other nine that he has edited or translated), his one hundred and fifty academic papers, lectures, book chapters or pamphlets, and several boxes full of his sermons and addresses, book reviews, newspaper articles, forewords and other occasional pieces. And it is not simply the number of these words that is formidable: they are often arranged in mindachingly complicated patterns. Williams himself speaks of his 'constipated and abstract words',[1] and although that is harsh self-criticism for a writer who is frequently elegant and normally measured and orderly, there is no doubt that the orchestration of his writing is sometimes bewildering, and unapologetically so.

Williams warns at one point that we should not expect to avoid this academic kind of difficulty, and that we should not sentimentalize simplicity: reality *is* complex, and we should not be surprised to find that complex thinking is needed to do justice to it. If that means struggling one moment with the most massive of nineteenth-century German philosophers, the next with the tantalizing fragments left by a fourth-century heretic, the next with sixteenth-century mystical theologians or an abstruse twentieth-century ethicist; if it means grappling with original sources in Byzantine Greek, in medieval Latin, in early modern Spanish, in modern Russian and French, and in Welsh; if it means developing an ability to work not just with dogmatic theology but with analytic philosophy, literary criticism, intellectual and social history; if it means following complex threads of argument which refuse to stay neatly linear and easily digestible; if it means following Marxist, Freudian, or postmodern critics as they lift the apparently simple paving slabs on which we're walking to show the quagmire underneath – well, so be it. The subject matter demands no less; Williams is dealing with something that 'does not instantly and effortlessly make sense'[2] – with questions that extend their prophetic, judging fingers into every messy area of our lives and our world. Acting responsibly toward this uncontrollable subject matter means acknowledging its real difficulty – and if there is a danger of elitism in Williams' enthusiastic embracing of this difficulty, he argues that there would be a different kind of elitism in hiding it away, in assuming that really complex topics should be kept behind locked doors where only the experts will see them, and where the simple faithful may be safe from them. The delight and beauty of real difficulty – of difficulty which leads us deeper into the inexhaustible depths of God, of difficulty which forces us to engage with the differences which the difficult Gospel makes in a bewildering world, of difficulty which upsets our illusionary sense of control – should be available to all.[3]

Of course, like almost any academic author, there are times when Williams' writing is *unduly* complicated, moments when it is weighted down with unnecessary jargon, or arguments which turn out to have twists and riffs that are purely decorative; he would be the first to admit this, and to admit that it is a failing. In one of his book reviews he criticizes another author for demanding 'exceptionally high levels of literacy in contemporary theoretical debate',[4] and suggests that a text which keeps its readers at bay in this way is not just stylistically but *morally* questionable; on the other hand he praises another author for his 'absence of what might be called intellectual tribalism (the sending out of signals by the use of jargon)'.[5] However difficult the subject-matter, an author has a duty to struggle towards what Williams calls a 'plain style': a way of presenting arguments and ideas which works to invite readers in, which strives to show them the springs and levers by which these arguments operate, and which tries not to topple them into submission by throwing around academic weight.[6] Certainly it is no failing to require patience, to require careful attention, to require *work* from one's readers; the problem arises when the difficulty is of a kind which *excludes* readers, however willing they may be to struggle to understand. There is a difference between what we might call *closed* and *open* difficulty – difficulty that excludes and bludgeons, on the one hand, and difficulty that invites in on the other. Although there are slips into closed difficulty, the main body of Williams' writing is characterized by *open* difficulty: by complex arguments and subtle conclusions laid out in demanding but, in principle, accessible ways, and by the assumption that this difficulty is open to exploration by anyone and everyone who cares about the subject matter.

So, Williams' writings are difficult in two distinct ways. Much of his writing exhibits real academic difficulty – difficulty of style, of range, of reference, of argument. Nevertheless, this academically difficult writing serves a simple message: all of it, that is, tries to proclaim the good news of God's utterly gracious, utterly gratuitous love, and raises the question of what difference that love makes to us. And that simple message is the most difficult one we can ever hear, in a rather different sense of 'difficult': it is difficult not because it will demand our most painstaking intellectual skills but because it will demand *everything*. The academic difficulty is important but secondary: it is necessary to do justice to the ramifications of the Gospel message, and it may be one way in which we *learn* the depth and seriousness of the Gospel demands – but academic difficulty is not inherent in the message itself. The real difficulty, the deep, disturbing challenge of the Gospel, is, on the other hand, inherent; it is unavoidable. If we do not hear *that* difficulty, we have not heard the Gospel.

It is my job to try to lead you around the hedges of Williams' academic difficulty – the difficulty of style, reference, jargon, and argument – and to try to show you the simple Gospel themes that stand at the centre of them all. In so doing, I hope that his academic difficulty will become easier to negotiate, and that the real challenge of his message, the real *Gospel* difficulty, will become clear.

III

This book will not, of course, tell you all that you need to know about Rowan Williams' theology. He chases implications of the Gospel through so many areas, and pursues them at such great depth and length, that in a short book like this I can't hope even to survey the territory he covers. If he were a famous tennis player, this book would not be a ball-by-ball description of even his most famous matches, nor an outline of his whole sporting career, but rather a sketch of the main shots that he puts together in any given game: his famous backhand, his cross-court pass, his top-spin lob. In any given match, Williams puts together this repertoire in creative and unpredictable ways, and often subtly hones each that he uses – responding to that particular oppo-nent on that particular day in those particular conditions. His characteristic shots are nevertheless recognizable and regularly repeated across many matches, and it is my aim to describe them simply and accessibly.

There is another sense in which this book's ambition is limited, however. It is not simply that I can't hope to do more than sketch some of the most familiar paths that Williams treads in his writ-ings. In addition, there is something strange about the choice to concentrate only on those writings in the first place, because it could fairly be said that much of his theology is found in places other than the printed page. He once wrote:

> There are moments when I am tempted to think that the only useful and honest moral discourse is in the context of confes-sion or direction, when the particularities of experience are brought slowly into connection with the communally-confessed truth of God's nature and activity.[7]

What he says here about 'moral discourse' could be said about his theology as a whole: he is tempted to think that the only truly honest and useful theology that he can do is not going to be produced in the pages of public writings, ready to be read anywhere and everywhere by anyone who can get hold of them, but will only emerge in his thoughtful, practical engagement in particular times and places – particular situations where, as in confession or spiritual direction, he is making connections with specific lives. As the phrasing of the quotation suggests, this is

putting it too strongly, but I do think it true that much of what
he has written is best thought of as preparation – vital, unavoidable preparation, perhaps, but preparation all the same. There is
something *preliminary* about much of it: a sense that it tells you
a good deal about what it would be like to think theologically
about some topic or other, but that it does not fully commit itself
to thinking many particular topics all the way through – with
all the risk and vulnerability that such commitment implies.
There are some obvious exceptions: as an historian, Williams
has fully committed himself to patient and detailed involvement
in debates about the Christian Church in the fourth century,
arguing firmly and in detail for controversial conclusions, returning to the debates again and again. More accessibly, he has (as
we will be seeing) written very directly and forcefully on peace,
and is beginning to do so more regularly on various issues to do
with schools – in these cases going decisively beyond discussions
of *how* one makes appropriate contributions to such debates,
beyond the description of ground rules and resources for these
contributions, and into the risky business of making such contributions directly and forcefully. Nevertheless, the main places in
which Williams builds on the preparations set out in his main
writings, the main ways in which he goes beyond preparation
and risks vulnerable involvement in the messy business of making and defending specific proposals, are not in those writings
themselves: they are in the confessional, in relationships of spiritual direction, on the tarmac of an American military base,[8] in
extended conversation with the Primates of the Anglican Communion, in tutorials with students, and in his ministry as a priest,
bishop, and archbishop.

IV

What kinds of writings are we exploring? They are very varied
indeed, and it is difficult to give any kind of overview. They are
writings which not only treat a very wide variety of topics, but
which speak in a variety of markedly different *registers* (that

is, addressing different audiences, for different purposes, using different 'tones of voice'). Despite this diversity, there is also a certain pervasive *character* to Williams' writings, and a remarkable level of deep *coherence*, in the sense that nearly all his writings emerge from, and contribute to, a coherent theological vision. When preparing to write this book, I turned from some of Williams' most recent writings to his earliest published work and found that, despite differences in style and approach, I was on familiar territory: the theological vision (though perhaps less developed, less richly orchestrated) was entirely recognizable. In the remainder of this introductory chapter, we'll look at those three things in turn: the *character*, *register* and *coherence* of Rowan Williams' writings.

My favourite illustration of the character of Williams' work comes from the title of an article he wrote in 1984. An important piece in which he set out the real differences between his own position and that of a controversial popular theologian, it was called, 'On not *quite* agreeing with Don Cupitt'.[9] Characteristically, Williams explored all the territory that he did share with Cupitt, and gave Cupitt's challenge to his own work as sympathetic a hearing as he could, before setting out calmly, quietly and clearly his remaining questions about Cupitt's project. The tone is persistently humble, sympathetic, *irenic* – that is, peace-loving, peace-making; Williams does not simply charge in assuming that he is right, and run Cupitt's work against a checklist of correct opinions. He listens carefully; he tries to hear the challenge inherent in the other person's work; he tries to discover common ground. And when, following all that, he still has criticisms or questions, they have all the more force: that article is, in my opinion, one of the more devastating critiques of Cupitt's theology available. Of course, Williams' irenic attitude sometimes falters. In 1998, for instance, he condemned some of the work of Jack Spong as based on 'a level of confusion and misinterpretation that I find astonishing', saying, 'I cannot in any way see Bishop Spong's theses as representing a defensible or even an interesting Christian future'; much earlier, in a 1976 book-review, with sweeping scorn, he had dismissed most of his theological contemporaries with the words, 'Time was when Anglo-Saxon philosophy held the palm for Philistine triviality; Anglo-Saxon theology now shows every sign of following this distinguished example.'[10] However, these brief and isolated ventures into more vitriolic territory have all the more bite because they *are* isolated, and because elsewhere the tone is pervasively irenic. And this peace-seeking style is no accident: as we shall be seeing, peace (in a sense which includes the conduct of debate between theologians) is a central concern of Williams' theology.

Williams also characteristically pays attention to detail. That is, he looks for ways in which generalizations and sweeping statements can be tripped up by awkward particulars. When laying out big conceptual mattresses, he is always trying to feel for the recalcitrant pea that refuses to be smoothed away. (This, by the way, accounts for some of the academic difficulty of his writing: like celebrities surrounded by minders, most clear statements of his ideas are accompanied immediately by a phalanx of qualifications – try to focus on the idea too quickly and you're quite likely to end up with a picture of a minder's hand, blocking your view.) To some extent, Williams is academically most at home not with the big statements of philosophy, but with the painstaking attention to detail of history: working with extraordinary care through, say, the masses of unruly evidence that remain to us from fourth-century theological debates, trying to undermine any too-easy telling of the story. This, too, is no accident: it is deeply connected to Williams' theology of the Incarnation, and to his recommendation of contemplation (of paying attention to what we do not control), as we shall see.

The final characteristic to notice is Williams' constant mixing of theology, spirituality and politics. One moment, Williams can be discussing the meaning of 'one substance' in the Nicene Creed, the next he will be discussing the 'dark night of the soul' experienced in prayer, and the next the economic and social problems posed by globalization. He refuses to acknowledge sharp boundaries between these areas of conversation – constantly showing, in fact, that there are deep and telling connections between them. Another way of putting this is to say that you are seldom *safe*

when reading Williams' work. Whenever you think you are
reading about something distant and controllable – a dry tech-
nicality, a thin philosophical abstraction, an ancient historical
debate – the ground can suddenly shift, and you find yourself
confronting an uncomfortable insight into your capacity to
deceive yourself, or an awkward exposure of the connections
between your domestic actions and world poverty, or the abuse
of children. Or you think you are safely embroiled in a question of spirituality, exploring personal territory that is deeply
familiar, only to discover not only that your attitudes to global
economics are being brought into the discussion but that you're
also expected to connect all this to deep, abstract metaphysical
commitments you did not know you had. Williams' work is
constantly crossing boundaries, in the confidence that the Gospel
has crossed them before him.

That crossing of boundaries is related to another feature of
Williams' work. He says in the prologue to an important collection of essays published in 2000 that they are 'a bit unstable in
register' – by which he means that his writings differ markedly
in their intended audiences, and in their apparent aims.[11] The
variety is partly explained by the fact that so much that Williams
has written is occasional – that is, commissioned for a specific
audience for a specific event. He seldom sits down to write on a
topic of his own choosing, for general publication. The variety
goes more deeply than this, however, and Williams suggests that
his writings vary according to whether the 'celebratory', the
'communicative' or the 'critical' mood is uppermost.

   Think of it this way. Williams writes as a Christian theologian,
and so as an inheritor of a vast quantity of Christian thinking,
speaking, acting, and writing – of the whole of what he sometimes calls Christian 'language', meaning much more by that than
spoken or written Christian *words*. He finds himself working in
a context where Christian 'language' is alive in worship and mission, and much of his work simply explores this language, examining the ways in which it points towards and flows from the
cross and resurrection of Christ, and towards the unfathomable

love of God. That is, he attempts to find the deep patterns and structures which hold that language together, and to explore just how widely it reaches, how deeply it goes. He refers to this as his 'celebratory' work: the work of exploring and delighting in the structures of the language he has inherited.

At other times, however, he concentrates more on the fact that this Christian language is spoken in our world alongside a whole range of other languages – the languages of other religions, the languages of secular morality and politics, the languages of uncommitted popular culture, and so on. He can concentrate on discovering connections between these languages, immersing himself in those other languages to see where they might be open to, or might resemble, or might be interestingly different from, Christian language. There's often something playful about this – Williams refers to it as 'experimenting' with these other languages: playing around with them, and *suggesting* ways in which they might appropriately connect with Christian language. He refers to this as his 'communicative' work – and notes that it is sometimes when one is experimenting in this way with non-Christian language that one gains a new perspective on Christian language itself, and is able to see things about it that had become invisible from the inside.

Lastly, Williams speaks about doing 'critical' work. Celebratory work tends to assume that Christian language, as we've inherited it, is working just fine. Sometimes, whether during the explorations involved in celebratory work, or with the strange perspectives that communicative work allows, one might see that there is at least a question about whether Christian language is whole and healthy – a question about whether it needs *repair*. And that sends one back to the deep sources of Christian language, to its fundamental claims, its fundamental visions, to ask how they suggest we go about that repair. 'Critical' work assumes that Christian language is not finished and complete, but is still in the process of being made – and that it can only be properly made by means of constant return to the sources that generate it. Christian language is not simply an undivided whole, which one either accepts whole and uncriticized, or abandons completely.

It is a language which points to certain things as central, as deter-
minative – as criteria by which the whole can be judged. 'The
Church', Williams says, 'lives under judgement: its empirical
condition is always to be thought through, tested in the light of
the reality to which its existence is supposed to bear witness.'
And 'A Church without the thinking and speaking of the underlying nature of its common life is in danger of muffling the critical
energy that is in reality always at work in it.'[12] Williams notices,
however, that by requiring us to think about the connection of
Christian language to its generative sources, and by leading us
to see it as flowing, however fallibly, from those sources, 'critical' work pushes us back towards 'celebratory' – towards the
delighted exploration of the structures of Christian language.[13]
Nevertheless, 'critical' work is not simply identical to 'celebratory'
work, and in some moods Williams can say, 'The theologian's
job may be less the speaking of truth . . . than the patient diag-
nosis of untruths, and the reminding of the community where its
attention begins.'[14]

Although he relates to it in different ways in his 'celebratory',
'communicative', and 'critical' moods, there is a constant and
coherent Christian vision in Williams' work – a vision of what
is essential about Christian language, a vision of what are the
deepest internal sources of critique and judgement in Christian
language. In a 1995 article, Williams examines the claim of Don
Cupitt that 'Under modern conditions . . . a theologian has got to
be a heretic'[15] – that is, the theologian has to explore boldly new
religious insights that, although they may allow us to salvage
something of our religious language, will prompt us to fearless
revision of that language to make it meaningful for a modern
audience. Williams contrasts this with the alternative suggestion
of Michael Ramsey that theology rests on what Williams calls
a 'non-negotiable . . . central complex of commitments' – commitments without which theology is impossible. Williams sides
clearly and firmly with Ramsey: his is 'the only rationale, finally,
for theology'.[16] There is in Christian language, however obscured
it may sometimes become, at least a glimpse of a vision of God's

universal love active in the world in the life, death, and resurrection of Jesus of Nazareth – and a commitment to the nature of God *as* love shown in that activity, and to the love to which we are called in response to that activity. This vision is, for Christian theology, a given; it is a gift: it is that which enables theology to function, and that on which theology goes to work; it is that which theology attempts to understand more deeply. In critical mood as much as in celebratory, theology is the attempt to do justice to this central vision of the love of God enacted in Jesus of Nazareth. And in all the registers of Rowan Williams' work, one thing is clear: very early on in his work, he arrived at some kind of grasp of how this deep vision hung together – something like a *feeling* for this vision as a whole – and all his work since has been directed towards exploring and refining that basic sense, in the conviction that this vision 'offers a sufficient imaginative resource for confronting the entire range of human complexity without evasion or untruthfulness'.[17] The remainder of this book is intended simply to sketch in the outline of this coherent vision, and to point to ways in which the reader may, with Williams' help, explore it further.

Chapter One

Disarming Acceptance

I

Jacob was a man who made a life out of running away.[1] When he had stolen the blessing due to his elder brother Esau, establishing himself at his brother's expense, he fled to the land of his uncle Laban, out of earshot of his brother's murderous threats. Years later, once he had taken from Laban more than Laban intended to give, we see him fleeing back again – desperate to put distance and a fixed boundary between himself and his uncle's resentment. The second flight, however, brought him back towards Esau, and as soon as his brother loomed larger in his mind than his uncle – as soon, that is, as he heard that his brother was on his way to meet him, surrounded by his men – Jacob began to panic once again, 'greatly afraid and distressed', thinking that his brother 'may come and kill us all'. Jacob had prospered on his stolen blessing, but now he nervously spent what he had gained in an attempt to buy safety. He made elaborate defensive preparations, dividing his company in two so that one half at least might be able to escape in an attack, and then sending his servants towards Esau driving two hundred and twenty goats, the same number of sheep, fifty cattle, thirty camels, and as many donkeys – telling each servant to explain to Esau that these were presents for him from his anxious brother. Jacob armed himself with all the substance he had acquired, fighting to turn away Esau's anger.

But Esau ran to meet him, embraced him, fell on his neck and kissed him, refusing the unwanted appeasing gifts; he stepped past all the defensive preparations, past all the history that lay between him and his brother, and unexpectedly, gratuitously, accepted him. Jacob, all his elaborate preparations undone, wept in his brother's arms. And in the brief opening that Esau's unexpected generosity created, Jacob became a theologian. He said to his brother, 'Truly, to see your face is like seeing the face of God, since you have received me with such favour.' In Esau's disarming acceptance – this gratuitous, undeserved, unearned acceptance, acceptance that swept away all the attempts which Jacob had made to secure it, acceptance which made a new future possible despite the tangled history that lay behind them – Jacob recognized the likeness of God.

Jacob's entire self was built from deceits, strategies, negotiations, and defensiveness. He had learnt this from his mother, and had practised it in all his encounters: snatching what he could from life, and running from the consequences. That was simply who he now was, and we see no hint of any buried resources that might help him become a different kind of person; even in the midst of their encounter, Jacob tried to win Esau over by offering him further gifts, and by calling him 'my lord'. But Esau responded, 'I have enough, *my brother*.' Esau reminded him that not everything can be negotiated, that he loved him because of the givenness of the blood relationship between them, rather than because of anything Jacob had managed to earn or coerce. And this reminder of a relationship deeper than negotiation, deeper than defence and coercion, acted as a judgement upon the self that Jacob had built, the self that he had become. It marked that self out as unnecessary, as destructive, as an obstacle to the recognition of this true relation.

Yet Jacob, it seems, could not fully accept Esau's sincerity. He wept; he recognized the face of God in Esau's face – but he did not stop negotiating. Apparently still worrying that Esau was acting only to further his own advantage, Jacob refused to call Esau 'brother', and kept up his strategic use of the language of 'lord' and 'servant'; he urged his gifts upon Esau again, and made his excuses so that they need not travel too far together. No common future was built upon the moment of clarity and recognition that Esau's generosity had allowed, and the last that we hear is that the land proved insufficient to support both of them, and that Esau with all his wives and children and livestock and property moved to a place 'some distance from his brother Jacob'. The two men continued to relate as rivals, as competitors, unable to find a common good in a land of limited resources; they did not find a way of living together as brothers, held together by a bond deeper than competition. Esau's disarming acceptance of his brother, which undermined and judged the defensive stratagems from which Jacob had built his life, was not allowed to do its transformative work.

II

The illustration is mine, but for Rowan Williams the Gospel is very like the glimpse of God's face which Jacob saw in the face of his brother Esau. It is a message of disarming acceptance – the news that we are held by a gratuitous love which undermines and overthrows the selves we have built from defensiveness and calculation. We have been met by a love which steps over all the boundaries we have scratched around the territory we call our own, all the ways we have of deploying our substance to negotiate a position in the world, all the subtle stratagems we use to protect ourselves against rejection. We are accepted by a love which is non-negotiable, as unavoidable as a blood relationship, and so by a love which we can neither secure nor avoid: a love in the face of which our manoeuvring and bargaining are irrelevances. It is a love, we might say, that exposes and condemns the acquisitive, defensive, strategic 'self' we have created.

So this is good news that crucifies us. The message of this unearned acceptance works upon us like an acid, eating away at our defensiveness, our terror of exposure, our fear of failure, our 'dread of having our powerlessness nakedly spelled out for us';[2] it undermines the false solidity we have given ourselves; it erodes the 'nightmares of guilt and insecurity which paralyse our imagination';[3] it saps the deep belief that our place in the world is something to be 'laboriously perfected, precariously possessed and violently defended'.[4] The Gospel eats away at the foundations of our self-understanding, our understanding of others, and our understanding of the world – understandings which have been built on the sand of an ultimate insecurity.

We are, all of us, precarious creatures. We live in environments we cannot control, and are hedged about by limits we cannot overcome. We face frustration, we face competition for scarce resources, and we are jostled in a confined space by the egos of others. There is only a limited difference that we can make, and we have only a limited control over even that difference; our actions are inevitably shaped by what others have done to us, and they mix uncontrollably with the actions of others and the unpredictable resistances of our environment, and they escape us. Our unavoidable dependence on and involvement with others is distorted by their selfishness, and the inevitable dependence of others on us and their involvement with us is distorted by ours. And in the midst of all this, we constantly invent ways of pretending that all of this is not true, or of refusing the responsibility with which it leaves us. We inherit and invent endless ways to deny our finitude. We ruffle our feathers to make ourselves big enough to scare the world; or we try to move the world to pity us. We try to force the world to feel its moral obligation towards us, or we try to make ourselves so small that the world will not notice us. We pretend that we can shape the world to our will, or we despair and assume that we make no difference at all, and that we are therefore not responsible. We are finite, we are mortal, we are weak – and in the absence of any sure foundation, these truths are too bitter for us, and we hide them behind layers and layers of fantasy and illusion. We try to persuade ourselves that there is some territory in the world, or some core to our selves, in which we alone are in control, in which we alone get to define what is valuable. We scratch away at the world to produce some space in it that is definitively *ours*, that we can defend against all comers – knowing that, deliberately or inadvertently, imperceptibly or violently, others would colonize it if they could.

'The Gospel', says Williams, 'frees us from fear and fantasy

. . . it is the great enemy of self-indulgent fantasy.'[5] The Gospel is the message that we are held in a loving regard which we cannot coerce or fight off, and which has no shadow of selfishness about it – no shadow of our being co-opted into somebody else's strategies, somebody else's fantasy. And so it is the message that we are set free to see and to accept our finitude, our limitation, our mortality, and to surrender that finite, limited, mortality to the love which upholds us. Because the Gospel assures us that we are held by a love which invites us truly to be ourselves, we discover that we do not need to carve out, fence round, and defend any other kind of space in the world; we do not need to throw up walls to keep out the barbarians. But recognizing and welcoming this Gospel 'is a hard and frightening task',[6] and we fight against the 'pain and disorientation' of this enlightenment.[7] As Williams puts it in *The Wound of Knowledge*, learning to hear the Gospel calls for a 'readiness to be questioned, judged, stripped naked and left speechless'.[8] By asking us to forget that we 'have a self to be shielded, reinforced, consoled and lied to',[9] it calls us to let that old self die.

To believe in this loving acceptance is to know this self to be judged and overturned; to hear this 'Yes' is to hear a 'No' to the current shape of our lives. And so the Gospel comes to us as a gift and as a task, or rather a gift that is a task. It comes to us as a completely free, utterly gratuitous, totally unearned gift, with the givenness of a wholly loving relation – but it is nevertheless a gift that we have to *learn* to accept, if we are not, like Jacob, to walk away from it, taking our possessions with us. In older Christian language, the Gospel is an inextricable mix of 'justification' (the news that we are accepted, despite our unworthiness) and 'sanctification' (the total reshaping of our broken, defensive lives to make them reflections of this gratuitous love, which is our learning of what this free acceptance means). This is a Gospel we can only respond to with both gratitude and a deep openness to being judged and remade.

III

Jacob and Esau failed to build a common good together. They remained in competition for scarce resources, each setting boundaries which kept the other out – until one of them was forced to leave the land and go elsewhere, leaving the other as victor. They found themselves unable to relate as brother and brother, but rather were caught in a different level of relation, where each sat uneasily on the edge between 'lord' and 'slave', playing a game in which they had to become one or the other, a game in which there had to be a winner and a loser.

The glimpse of a different way of relating that Jacob had seen in Esau's God-like welcome was not simply a glimpse of a transformed self for Jacob: a wonderful but terrifying glimpse of a life in which he would no longer need to fight for position. It was also a glimpse of a different kind of corporate future – a future in which the two brothers would belong together, and in which it simply would not make sense to think in terms of a potential winner and a potential loser.

If the first question that Rowan Williams' understanding of the Gospel puts to us is 'What difference does it make to my self-understanding if I believe myself to be held in a loving, accepting gaze?', the second question is, 'What difference does it make to our understanding of how we might live together if we believe that *each* of us is held in the same loving regard?' The Gospel enables us to discover ourselves, and it also 'makes possible new levels of belonging together in the human world' teaching us that 'our "kin" is a far odder and larger community than we could ever have expected'.[10] Jacob and Esau, having failed to think permanently as brothers, can only imagine a future in terms of the parcelling out of resources, in terms of the fixing of boundaries behind which each of them may hold sway, and behind which each of them has territory from which he can ensure that the other is excluded. What would it have meant for them to start thinking differently, to start imagining a common future, a future as *brothers*?

There is no easy answer. To think as brothers would not automatically remove the scarcity of resources. It would not automatically mean that the land would be able to support more livestock or more grain. And it would not be safe: Jacob, after all, is perfectly sensible to think that Esau might be using the language of 'brother' simply as a stratagem, a cunning move on the way to revenge. And Esau would be just as sensible to think that, had Jacob accepted the language of 'brother', he would find a way to twist the situation to his own ends, as he twisted everything that came into his hands. The love which Jacob and Esau glimpse, but from which they turn away, is not an easy solution or a set of neat answers. As soon as we start trying to think about it realistically, it begins to look thoroughly questionable. Nevertheless, the Gospel pushes its own question at us in response: aren't our normal ways of seeing this questionability, ways which assume the primacy of competition, exclusion, insecurity, and violence, themselves part of the problem?

The Gospel message is, for Williams, not simply one which percolates down into the lower reaches of our psyche, loosening the knots which have held us in place and enabling us to live with a new kind of freedom as mortal creatures in an overwhelming world. It is, also, unavoidably social: it forces us to rethink the ways in which we organize our relations with others – family, friends, neighbourhood, nation, world. None of our relationships are left untouched by this Gospel, and it cannot remain a personal or private matter. The Gospel is unavoidably *political*.

IV

Already the ramifications and implications are beginning to spiral out of control, and topics have emerged that are going to need whole chapters of their own before we are even clear how to *begin* dealing with them. However, before turning to exploring the transformation of the self (Chapter Four) and of society (Chapter Five) to which this message of disarming acceptance calls us, we need to examine a serious deficiency in the account given so far. The Gospel is a message of disarming acceptance, a message of crucifying love. But who is it that accepts us? Who is it that loves us? After all, the Gospel is not, for Williams, a self-help mantra that we repeat to ourselves in the mirror every morning, a message that we create and control, and can modify to suit our felt needs. Nor is it a message about a generalized, abstract idea of love, distilled on a laboratory bench or in a theologian's study. It is not the message that we are loved by nobody in particular, or that we can and should love ourselves. It is a message from beyond us; it is a message that we hear but do not own, a message which always retains the power to challenge and upset our understanding of it; it is a message that has a particular shape which we do not control, and which we must painstakingly learn. But where or who does it come from?

We may begin answering this question by looking at how the Gospel first emerged. As Jacob heard an echo of this Gospel when confronted by Esau's face so, Williams says, the first Christians heard the Gospel not when they invented a message of love to sooth themselves, but when they were addressed or called out of themselves by Jesus of Nazareth. His whole life was the message of disarming acceptance to them. 'Foxes have holes, and birds of the air have nests; but the Son of Man has nowhere to lay his head,' said Jesus.[11] He did not seek to make and defend any space for himself, but gave himself over for the sake of others' flourishing. He refused to coerce from the world a position for himself or a future for his followers. He gave himself completely to those around him, stepping past ritual and social boundaries, and past boundaries erected by actual wrongdoing, to call men and women his brothers and sisters, his friends – setting no conditions upon his regard. In his healings, he approached those whose ailments removed them from full membership in society, and drew them back; he did not hesitate to touch those who were unclean, stepping away from any claim to be clean himself in order that they might be cleansed. He ate with tax collectors and sinners, and even Pharisees, refusing to keep separate from them; allowing the challenge and difficulty of his message to emerge from his free fellowship with them all. And he attacked the central means by which full membership in his society was brokered: the temple and the priesthood, which preserved and regulated the core practices of his society, making access to them possible, but at the same time inevitably setting conditions upon that access, parcelling it out according to criteria. And so he inevitably suffered the fate of any who live with such abandon in a world like ours: he was found to be a troublemaker, one who undermined the divisions and exclusions which allowed his world to tick over – and he was killed, by an alliance of religious and political power. But he refused to run even from death, refused even then to defend his territory, and gave himself over, making a gift of his life.

Above all, when his followers had abandoned him, had apostatized and betrayed him, giving him over to this death in order to preserve their own lives, he did not give them up but returned to them and forgave them. Jesus, who had been betrayed, handed over, tortured, and crucified, returned to his betrayers and his torturers, still bearing the marks of their betrayal and their violence, still as the crucified one, and once again stepped over the barrier that their rejection and abandonment had created between themselves and him – and offered them his love, his acceptance. He, their victim, offered them forgiveness and the possibility of transformation, creating with them a community of forgiven people. The resurrection, says Williams, creates forgiven persons, in a community of the forgiven.[12] We see this in the account in Acts, as the resurrection of Jesus is proclaimed in Jerusalem to those who arranged his death – yet not as the unexpected arrival of vengeance, casting down those who had cast him down, but as a message of forgiveness and of hope. And we see it in John's Gospel, in the description of the encounter of Simon Peter with the crucified Jesus in Galilee, in which Peter is reminded of his betrayal of Jesus on the night of Jesus' arrest – and forgiven. In the words which Jesus speaks to him we see that

> Peter's fellowship with the Lord is not over, not ruined, it still exists and is alive because Jesus invites him to explore it further . . . To know that Jesus still invites is to know that he accepts,

forgives, bears and absorbs the hurt done: to hear the invitation is to know oneself forgiven, and *vice versa*.[13]

Not even direct and deliberate denial of their Lord is enough to move the disciples beyond the sphere in which he offers his loving fellowship.

Yet although this was an acceptance without conditions, it was not an acceptance which made no demands. Rather, it demanded everything. To follow Jesus, he makes clear, is to lose one's life in order to find it; it is to tread the way of the cross. Jesus stepped over all the boundaries which those around him had erected, even the boundary made by betrayal and death, and came close to them again – but his was not a comfortable presence. It was a presence which did not so much answer their questions as put *them* to the question, forcing them to see in an unwelcome light the rotten stuff from which their lives were made.[14] And so the disciples, gratuitously chosen and freely loved, do not have an easy time in the Gospels, but repeatedly (even after the resurrection) have their grasp of the situation tugged from them by Jesus' refusal to trundle neatly along the grooves which they have laid for him.

The disarming love of the Gospel, the love which generates true life, which strips away illusion and calls us to our true identity – Jesus' early followers found that love active and unimpeded in him. They found when they met him that this love grasped them and would not let them go. This love was not simply a message that he brought, as if he were a philosopher teaching about an abstract ethic of love; the disciples did not receive the message and then take it away to ponder in their own time. Rather Jesus embodied this message in his life among them. He lived this love towards them, responding to their particular betrayals and failures with a resourceful love that continued to make a common future possible. In the concrete shape of his life among them, they found the Gospel question posed to them unavoidably, in an historical, living form – a form lived all the way to death. They found themselves put to the question by Jesus' life with them, and judged by his loving acceptance of them. What difference does it make to be loved like this?

V

As it stands, this could be simply another *illustration* of the Gospel message – like the story of Jacob and Esau, an example which helps us to grasp something of the nature of the Gospel, but which is itself ultimately dispensable. As an illustration it would be a useful, but not a necessary, way in to the truth; the touching story at the beginning of a sermon. If this were so, then we might certainly say that what we saw partially in Esau (a love which steps over injury to create the possibility of a new future) we see more fully in Jesus, but we would also have to say that the lesson we learn is as detachable from Jesus as it is from Esau. Were we to say this, however, we would once again be faced with a Gospel message telling us that we are loved by nobody in particular, and it would begin to sound all too like a story which we are told only by ourselves, a message which we can grasp and own and control, because we do not have to answer for it to any reality beyond ourselves. And it would begin to look more and more like one of the illusory ways we have of securing and defending our position in the world, spinning fantasies to hide the stark truth of our homelessness from our anxious minds. The Gospel would begin to look like part of the problem, not a message about the answer.

No, says Williams: the Christian Gospel does not work like this. In order to understand how it does work, however, we need to remove a restriction which I have artificially imposed on the way I have told the story of Jesus so far: we need to talk about Jesus' relationship to *God*. Jesus, after all, constantly described his work as obedience, as a carrying out of his Father's will; he constantly directed his disciples' attention away from himself and towards the source from which his actions flowed. And the disciples found him transparent to God's light. When Jacob was greeted by Esau and saw in his face the face of God, he proved unable, eventually, to accept the challenge that Esau's greeting represented. However much this was due to the ingrained nature of his mistrust, it also has something to do with Esau himself.

This is, after all, the same brother who had made murderous threats against Jacob – a brother who might plausibly be thought still to be seeking revenge, or even simple redress. The face of God could only shine faintly in Esau's face, for Jacob, and there could be no escaping the suspicion that it was a mask for darker intentions. Christianity arises from the early disciples' conviction that in Jesus of Nazareth the face of God was unclouded; facing Jesus, they could say without faltering, 'To see your face is to see the face of God', or 'We have seen his glory, the glory as of a father's only son, full of grace and truth':[15] full of the grace which loves freely, and the truth which exposes our darkness.

Jesus emerges against a particular background, among a particular people who spoke a particular language about God, and it is only possible to understand the sense which his first followers made of him, and which he made of himself, if we see how he related to, and transformed, the ways of thinking and speaking about God which were his and their inheritance. Williams draws our attention in particular to the ways in which the Jewish understanding of God was tied to experiences of 'transformation or renewal of such scope that they can only be ascribed to an agency free from the conditions of historical contingency' – experiences which had pushed the Jewish people beyond the idea that they had to deal with multiple gods, beyond the idea that they were worshipping one god amongst many, beyond the idea that their god was tied to the fortunes or failings of one nation, and towards the idea that the one whom they met in the Exodus or in Exile was the one God who upheld the whole world.[16] And Williams also notes that, whatever temptation there might have been for Israelites to see this God simply as the supernatural wing of their own army, defending what they chose to uphold, they were in fact constantly called to account, constantly unsettled and transformed in their encounters with him. God, in Judaism, constantly refused to be domesticated.

Jesus' followers, breathing this atmosphere, experienced in the specific, finite life of the man from Nazareth a transformation or renewal that refused to stay limited to his specific time and place – refused to be bound by 'the conditions of historical contingency'; and they experienced a transformation or renewal that cut at the roots of their understanding of themselves, of other people, and of the world. Jesus' impact – the impress which his life, death and resurrection made on those around him, and on those to whom they proclaimed him – was experienced against this background as *divine* action. God is the one who redeems from slavery; in Jesus, the disciples experienced a release from slavery more complete than the Exodus or the return from Exile. God is the one who creates the world; in Jesus, the disciples experienced a re-creation, a bringing of creation to fruition, which they could only ascribe to that same generative, creative power. God is the one who calls all things to judgement, whose word establishes and casts down; in Jesus, the disciples experienced a judgement which divided their bones from their marrow. And so they could say that 'Jesus is the form which God's judgement takes.'[17]

Jesus' disciples believed that they had encountered in him – and that they continued to encounter in him – an unfettered love, a piercing judgement: a love and judgement of universal scope. They believed that there was no chamber of their lives, no acre of their world, which was left untouched by what they had encountered in him; in the aftermath of his resurrection, they travelled to and beyond the edges of the world they knew, convinced that they would not reach the edges of his significance. It did not make sense to them to think of the acceptance which had met them in him being a love which applied only to the small group of those who had encountered Jesus during his ministry; they knew Jesus' reckless love as an acceptance which acknowledged no boundaries, and a judgement which could call any reality into question – an acceptance which forgave in the name of God, and a judgement which spoke with the voice of God. The heartbeat of their faith was therefore a conviction that 'a brief succession of contingent events in Palestine' judges 'every assertion about the significance of life and reality'.[18] In the particular words and gestures of this one life, they found a gateway into an overwhelming divine reality. As Williams puts it, the disciples looked at Jesus, and saw him '*coming out* from an immeasurable depth; behind or within him, infinity opens up . . . Belief in Jesus is seeing him as the gateway to an endless journey into God's love.'[19]

The Gospel which we see in Jesus' life tells us that we are held in *God's* loving regard. It is not a message we invent for ourselves each morning, hoping to shore up our flagging self-regard before facing another gruelling day; it is a message which tells us the deepest truth about ourselves. It is not a message about a lifestyle which we might choose to entertain; it is a message about the true source and end of human life – a message about the character of the one who holds us in being, the one who draws us onwards. The disciples did not believe that they had encountered simply one *option* for living in the world: a way appropriate to one particular group, but of no significance beyond its boundaries. Rather, they believed that in Jesus of Nazareth, they had touched bedrock. They believed that they had encountered 'the primary and irreducible *meaning* of what it is to be human, the fundamental context of human experience'. And, as such, what they said about Jesus began 'to take on more and more clearly the tone and character of what we say about God'.[20] Although they did not and could not cease to think of Jesus as the particular man from Nazareth (who had ministered among specific people at a specific time, who had died in a specific place, and who had been encountered as risen by specific people) they increasingly understood that this specific reality had upon them a transformative, generative, crucifying, and life-giving impact of divine depth and scope.

They understood Jesus as one whose life was uniquely saturated by the Gospel, entirely transparent to God's love.

When we listen to a great instrumental performer or singer, we can sometimes sense that all their energy and life at the moment of performance is held and sustained by the great current of music that is becoming present and immediate in their actions; you can't separate them from the movement of the music, their present reality, muscles and nerves and breath and mind, is shot through with the music's 'life'. They are carried on its tide.[21]

This, says Williams, is a 'small and inadequate analogy' for what Christians came to believe about Jesus: 'Jesus' human life is shot though with God's, he is carried on the tide of God's eternal life, and borne towards us on that tide, bringing with him all the full-ness of the creator.'[22] And Williams goes further:

> If Jesus is translucent to God in all he does and is, if he is empty so as to pour out the riches of God, if he is the well-spring of life and grace, what then? He *is* God; in infancy, in death, in eating and drinking, in healing and preaching . . . This is the Lord, God in flesh, God made known in history, God fear-ing, struggling and suffering; the only God we know or can know, the glory of God in the face of Christ, love and healing in human hands and eyes – how else could we grasp it?[23]

VI

So Christians find that they cannot speak about Jesus without speaking about God – without speaking about the divine scope of what takes place in him. But the opposite is also true: they find that they cannot speak about God without speaking about Jesus – without letting everything that they say about God be ground in the mill of Jesus' life, death, and resurrection.[24] The impact which he has upon them is such as to upset and transform all that they wish to say about God, and Christians find that their definitions of 'God' and 'Jesus' become inextricably tangled together.[25] It is not simply, then, that the disciples experienced in Jesus the action of a God they already understood clearly and fully, so that Jesus was simply a repetition of what they already knew. Rather, the disciples experienced Jesus as a decisive clarification, deepening, and transformation of their understanding of God – a decisive *revelation* of God.[26]

More can be said, however. If we turn to God, seeking to understand him directly, we find him pointing us to his Son. We might think of the words the Gospels portray as coming from heaven at Jesus' baptism or at the transfiguration, or we might think of Jesus' resurrection: 'God, in raising him, has said, "This is *my* work, *my* life: what is done in Jesus is what I do, now and always."'[27] Jesus is not simply one who happens to have lived in such a way as to show us what God is like; he is one who lives the life he does because God has chosen him to display God's life to the world – more than that, he is one who lives the life he does because God has chosen him to *enact* God's love within the world. From now on, the word 'God' is before anything else the name for the source of Jesus' life, the name for the deep reality which becomes visible in him,[28] and Jesus is 'God's own particular human reality by which in his love he identifies with all humanity' – he is God's way of loving the world.[29] The disciples did not meet in Jesus something which resembled God's love, or something which taught them what God's love was like; they did not simply encounter something which transformed their understanding of God's love: they encountered God's love itself. They encountered, in Jesus, God loving them.

We are still talking about a particular human life. We are talking about a finite man, with finite knowledge, finite powers, confined to one time and place. We are talking about a human being who grows and learns and develops within a particular context. To draw on terminology which I used earlier in this chapter, the Jesus about whom we are speaking is still to be understood as a 'precarious creature'. He lived in an environment he could not control, and was hedged about by limits he could not overcome. He faced frustration, he faced competition for scarce resources; he was jostled in a confined space by the egos of others. There was only a limited difference that his actions could make directly, and he had only a limited control over that difference; his actions were inevitably blended together in part from what others had done to him, and mixed uncontrollably with the actions of others and the unpredictable resistances of his environment, and so escaped him. He was unavoidably dependent on and involved with others. Jesus of Nazareth was fully, entirely, unreservedly human; a finite creature. And yet this finite, limited, creaturely humanity is the action of God, *is* God.

And so the appropriate attention to Jesus which lies at the

heart of Christianity cannot, primarily, be a focus on any errand achieved by Jesus which could be considered separately from his whole life, or which could have been performed equally by someone else; nor can the focus fall simply on the information that Jesus conveyed, if by that we mean a message that could have been carried by somebody else. Jesus is God's word to us not simply when he is speaking clearly, and not simply when he is acting intelligibly; Jesus is God's word to us when he is wrapped in swaddling cloths and placed in a manger, and when he is wrapped in grave clothes and placed in a tomb. Christian talk of incarnation directs our attention to the whole shape of Jesus' life; it is Jesus' *whole* life that is the Word of God. This fully human life, lived in a particular time and place, among a particular group of people, is God's word of acceptance and judgement for us; this messy, complex, human, finite, bounded reality, a life lived jostled by disciples, crowds, opponents – a life lived towards and on the cross – is God's face turned towards us.

Yet the disciples believed that, thanks to the resurrection, encounter with God's love in Christ was no longer limited to one time and place. So, on the one hand, we can affirm that Jesus lived God's love in his life, death, and resurrection not by communicating a general lesson about that love, but by loving people in particular ways – meeting them in their need and their deceit and their failure, and setting them on solid ground. He lived this love towards them in particular relationship to each of them, in a series of concrete encounters with them. And without the resurrection, all that would be available beyond this would be a kind of abstraction, a turning of the love which worked itself out in particular encounters and relationships into a general lesson that could be learnt well beyond the reach of such encounter. On the other hand, Christians believe that the resurrection has made encounter and relationship with Jesus available, in some sense, everywhere. Although by 'Jesus' we can only ever mean 'Jesus of Nazareth' – one particular human being who lived the love of God in one finite time and place – from as far back in Christianity as our historical analysis can carry us, Jesus has been regarded not as a dead exemplar, but as a living agent – as one who is still present in and beyond the believing community, and one who still mediates God's love to us.[30] We find ourselves compelled to say that this one finite life is

> free from local limitation, and free from the limitation of belonging to the past: without ceasing to be a particular person in a particular place, he is capable of interpreting an unlimited range of human situations . . . and there is no place or time or condition in which he can be domesticated, in which we can say that his story and his Spirit are exhaustively defined. He is utterly unsusceptible to definition; and while we may continue to burden him with our hopes, fantasies and projections, there is an obstinate and restless dimension of unclarity which will break through and challenge sooner or later.[31]

And so the love spoken of in the Gospel is a universal love, a love which meets anyone anywhere, but it is also an irreducibly particular love: a love that I learn fully only in the midst of a specific relationship with one who brings his whole self – crucified and risen – to bear on my whole self.

And the healing which the risen Jesus brings – the transforming effect of his acceptance – is not something complete and achieved all at once, as if his resurrection were simply the dispensable trigger for that healing, or a ladder that could be kicked down once it has been climbed. That healing is something that is worked out only in constantly repeated encounter with Jesus, as his disarming acceptance is repeatedly heard afresh and its meanings discovered in deeper areas of our lives, new areas of our world. As Williams puts it:

> Jesus grants us a solid identity, yet refuses us the power to 'seal' or finalize it, and obliges us to realize that this identity only exists in an endless responsiveness to new encounters with him in the world of unredeemed relationships.[32]

Because Jesus is alive, the Gospel of his love is not in our control; it is not in anyone's control but his own. Williams urges us to be alert to the subtle ways in which we manage to evade Jesus, and evade Jesus' challenge. He urges us to be aware of the ways in which we too easily try to assume control over this subject matter; the ways in which we too easily assume that we've *got it* – that we know what's going on, know how it works, and know what difference it should make. All these are ways in which we turn away from the kind of learning appropriate to a living relationship, and towards the kind of learning appropriate to memory of a dead exemplar. Williams urges us to be aware of the ways in which we can so concentrate on becoming masters of, or defenders of, particular conclusions about Jesus that we cease to hear him ourselves. To be centred on a living Jesus who lives beyond our grasp, beyond our memories and ideas and theories, is not to be centred on ourselves; it is not to be centred on our grasp of Jesus, or our conclusions about him, or our explanations of what took place through him. The Lordship of Jesus which Williams' work proclaims is the Lordship of a riddler, 'one who makes us strangers to what we think we know'.[33] It is the Lordship of one who constantly challenges and judges us – who whilst continually accepting and forgiving and healing us is in the very same action continually crucifying us.

'I can't see any way of being a Christian', Williams says, 'that doesn't involve you at some point saying that it is in relation to Christ that human beings become as human as they are meant to be'[34] – but we cannot turn that into self-glorification, and say either that *we* are now as human as we are meant to be (and that we have therefore gained all from Christ that we need to gain) or that it is only in relation to *our understanding* of Christ, our theologies, our proclamation, our control, that human beings become as human as they are meant to be. The tomb is empty; Jesus is alive, and he is out of our hands. 'Jesus is alive, he is there to be encountered again, and so his personal identity remains;'[35] he remains 'a person who obstinately stands over against us'.[36] The disciples, and all Christians, become carriers of the acceptance and the judgement that they have encountered in Jesus, not as people who live fully the gracious acceptance he has demonstrated (we remain ambiguous, conflictual, more Esau than

Jesus) nor as people who grasp fully the message they bear, but as those who point continually away from themselves and towards the living one in whom they trust. The righteousness which Christians take out into the world is Christ's, not their own.

The Gospel about which Williams talks is therefore never anything other than the Gospel of Jesus Christ – the Gospel which tells of his 'free, unanxious, utterly demanding, grown-up love', the Gospel which promises that we can 'receive from his fullness and set others free'. [37]

> Christ is the root of our security and our insecurity alike, promise and judgement, end and beginning, the burning bush, the Paschal lamb, the rock and the tabernacle, present as a sign of hope at every stage of our painful journey out of bondage and across the wilderness. [38]

The revelation which founds Christianity is not the revelation of a 'theory of everything', an intellectual or practical system which tells us everything worth knowing. It is, instead, the irrupting into historical life of God's pure, selfless love for us in Christ – that love which comes to us as a gift and as a question. We could think of Christianity as a voyage of discovery – a journey (or rather, thousands, millions, now billions of journeys) into all the corners of the world, of the psyche, of commerce, contemplation, conversation, by disciples bearing this question and asking, What difference does this make *here*? What is it to hear this question *now*? What would it be to believe the Gospel of Jesus Christ *here and now*? As Williams puts it, 'the meaning of Jesus is not the container of all other meanings but their test, judgement and catalyst'[39] – by which he means that Christians are not given, in Christ, a vast quantity of information about all the situations in which they will find themselves. Rather, they encounter the one foundational reality which will challenge, upset, and transform any situation in which they find themselves.

The Gospel question is not primarily one posed in the abstract by academic theologians; it is not carried to us on a bed of ideas, theories, and concepts: it is one borne by the life of a people called to carry and proclaim it, and it is one that this people has heard, and goes on hearing, in the life, death, and resurrection of Jesus of Nazareth. 'About twelve years ago,' Williams says, 'I was visiting an Orthodox monastery, and was taken to see one of the smaller and older chapels.'

> It was a place intensely full of the memory and reality of prayer. The monk showing me around pulled the curtain from in front of the sanctuary, and inside was a plain altar and one simple picture of Jesus, darkened and rather undistinguished. But for some reason at that moment it was as if the veil of the temple was torn in two: I saw as I had never seen the simple fact of Jesus at the heart of all our words and worship, behind the curtain of our anxieties and our theories, our struggles and our suspicion. Simply there; nothing anyone can do about it, there he is as he has promised to be till the world's end. Nothing of value happens in the Church that does not start from seeing him simply there in our midst, suffering and transforming our human disaster.[40]

The Gospel is not an abstract mantra, but an invitation 'to be drawn into cross and resurrection and to find *there* . . . at once a decisive No and an everlasting Yes to our selves'.[41]

VII

God's power 'works in the history of a human being betrayed and helpless, stripped of defence, of speech and action, and killed', a human being who refused to establish and defend any kind of resting-place in the world, or to demand any kind of easy consolation from God – and, says Williams, 'We understand the divine power to the degree that we enter into the same movement away from defence or security or mastery.'[42] So, although the Gospel is a message of gratuitous acceptance, of love lavishly and freely given, it is not a message of cheap consolation. It is not a message that promises to lift us above the bewildering world in which we live; not a message that promises to erase our mortality and finitude. It is not a message that promises to keep us from the cross. Williams refuses the idea that the Gospel is about a 'Christ who saves us the trouble of being crucified'[43] – the Christian is, rather, one who is baptized *into* the death of Christ, 'into his descent into hell, into a condition of vulnerability'.[44] From now on, in our attempts to understand God, 'all we have is the narrative of God with us . . . a narrative of [God's] "journey into a far country" . . . a story of God's Son as a creature and a mortal and defeated creature'.[45]

This is the unrelenting focus of Williams' discussions of the Gospels: the cross of Christ, which stands as a condemnation of all our attempts to secure for ourselves the kind of consolation, the kind of security, which Christ refused. Williams is painfully aware of the many ways in which we dilute this Gospel, trying to make it more palatable. We do not, it seems, wish to live with the implications of a loving acceptance so total, and so universal; we do not wish to see our defences and achievements bypassed and rendered irrelevant; we do not wish to be shown up as fearful and deceitful. We coat even the cross in sugar, and protect ourselves from the bitterness of the Gospel.

It sometimes seems that Williams is willing to risk muting the note of joy, of thankfulness, of release and rescue, appropriate to the news that God has stepped over all the barriers which separate us from him, and has accepted us despite ourselves. It sometimes seems that he is willing to risk rushing past this divine 'Yes' in order to slam the door closed on any easy Gospel, any message of cheap grace, which refuses the 'No' spoken on the cross. Any such Gospel, he says, is not the Gospel of Jesus Christ. If we have not heard the shattering 'No' of the Gospel – the judgement which falls upon our selfish and disordered lives, all our pretensions to a life which is safer than Jesus' life, a life which is stronger than Jesus' life, a life which is less precarious than Jesus' life – then we have not properly heard its all-encompassing 'Yes'.

We must ask, I think, whether the focus falls too consistently on the 'No' of the cross rather than on its encompassing 'Yes'. It is not that I can fault the logic: it is not, in other words, that I

believe Williams to have got the *shape* of the Gospel wrong. He is,
I believe, absolutely right, and absolutely orthodox, in his insistence that the Gospel's gratuitous acceptance always brings with
it disarming crucifixion. But I suspect that the tenor or atmosphere of his writing is too unrelentingly *agonized* – too aware of
the possibilities of self-deceit, too aware of the dangers of cheap
consolation, ever to relax in the Sabbath rest of God's love, feast-
ing at table with the Son, despite all the dangers that attend such
relaxation. As it stands, he runs the risk of proposing a kind of
spiritual heroism – not, of course, a heroism of successful and
achieved purity, but a heroism of open-eyed acknowledgement
of failure and finitude, a heroism of moral anguish; and it may
be that the only way of avoiding that pitfall is to balance this risk
with the risks of devout relaxation.

On the other hand, we must ask what implications his quite
proper passionate commitment to a difficult Gospel might have
in a Church which sometimes seems addicted to saccharine –
and ask whether it is our present situation, in a culture of quick
gratifications, which requires Williams to risk too great a focus
on the darkness of the Gospel. What delusory consolations might
this Gospel expose in our liturgies, our songs, our preaching, our
devotions, our outreach? What delusory consolations might it
expose in our leisure, our culture, our politics? These are questions which Williams believes we can never stop asking, because
our inventiveness in evading the cross is never-ending, and the
shattering work of the cross is never completed. Whatever my
questions about the balance of his presentation, I do not mean
to deny that to turn away too easily from these questions is to
turn away from the cross, and so to turn away from the Gospel.
It remains to be seen whether and how, in his tenure as Archbishop of Canterbury, his passion for the cross, his rejection of
easy grace, comes out in the guidance which he provides to the
Church of England and the wider Anglican Communion. If his
concern for the difficult Gospel of Jesus of Nazareth presses its
way beyond the academic difficulty of his writings, and begins to
worm its way into the Church at large, it may turn out that the
Anglican Church has taken on far more than it expected with

his appointment. I would like to think – perhaps naively – that we will one day be able to look back on this as the *real* challenge of his time in Canterbury. There is, after all, no challenge more vital.

Chapter Two

The Source of Life

I

In the months since September 11, 2001, an old cry against religion has come back with renewed and inevitable force. What can one say to somebody who insists that God has told them to kill? To what possible authority, court, or standard can one appeal that could call that belief to account? Even if we can make sense of the idea of questioning and correcting some person's *understanding* of God, isn't it a nonsense – for any religion that believes in a supreme God – to think of questioning and correcting *God*? And, therefore, doesn't all appeal to God, all talk of obedience to God, all ideas about surrender to God, feed the dark possibility of terrorism – by suggesting that we are meant to base our behaviour upon the dictates of a being beyond contradiction, beyond questioning, beyond standards? Doesn't any religion, in other words – at least, any religion which praises obedience to God or surrender to God – provide itself with a fatal gateway out of ethical behaviour and into atrocity? Isn't 'good' in such religions defined by what God chooses to command? And so doesn't any religion which praises obedience to God or surrender to God lay all the most important groundwork for those of its followers who end up believing that God is telling them to kill, and that such killing is good because God has commanded it?

These are serious questions, and we must not dismiss them too easily. But it is also important to analyse how the questions work, and what they understand by the word 'God'. In these questions, that word names an absolute and unimpeded *will* – a being or reality which may as it happens have decided to act in ways which we think good, and may even have promised to continue acting in such ways, but which only does so because it chooses to do so, with absolute freedom. Such a being's choice to be good is ultimately arbitrary – a matter of unconstrained decision, a decision above which there can be no higher court of appeal, a decision for which there can be no reasons, for all 'reasons' would be restraints upon this omnipotent will. In this picture, the arbitrary, absolute *will* of 'God' is primary; any *goodness* this 'God' happens to choose is secondary. We may speak of a 'loving God', but all that we can mean by this is 'an omnipotent being who happens to have chosen love', and so any obedience to this God is only secondarily and accidentally a commitment to love, primarily and definitively an obedience to absolute power. And so, yes, the antagonistic questioner is right: such obedience is always inevitably shadowed by the theoretical – and perhaps more than theoretical – possibility that this obedience to power could remain itself even if this power commanded something other than love. A terrorist can always appeal to God's power over God's love; the pacifist who believes in God has access to no higher court of appeal in which to call this power to account. Power trumps love, every time.

This definition of 'God' – as an omnipotent being, free to *choose* love – is, for Williams, turned upside-down by the Gospel. If Christian theology abides by what it learns in the disarming acceptance of Jesus of Nazareth – if 'God' is before anything else the name for the source of Jesus' life, the name for the deep reality which becomes visible in him – then we will simply not be able to understand God in the way those questions assume. The word 'God', in Christian theology, does not name a being or reality of unfettered power, who has *chosen* to love – it does not, that is, name a reality in which power goes deeper than love. Rather, it names a reality for whom – if I may put it like this – love goes all the way down. In the Christian picture, God's power always and only emerges from God's love – God's will from God's loving nature – and so love trumps power, every time. There is no shadow of power without love in God.[1]

The objector asks, 'In what court could we possibly bring God's arbitrary power to trial?' Williams can reply: in the court of the Gospel, in the court of Jesus of Nazareth. The Christian claim about incarnation, which we began to explore in the last chapter, means just this: that Jesus is the revelation – the transcription into the terms of our world, terms that we can read – of God's loving *nature*, of that source from which God's acts, God's power, God's will emerge. And this is part of what it means to say, as I did in the last chapter, that Christians 'find that they cannot speak about God without speaking about Jesus – without letting everything that they say about God be ground in the mill of Jesus' life, death, and resurrection': the revelation of God's nature in the life, death, and resurrection of Jesus of Nazareth *is* the revelation of our court of appeal.[2] Any turning away from that court of appeal to the shadow of a divine will unconstrained by it, or only arbitrarily and accidentally committed to it, is a turning away from the Christian meaning of the word 'God', towards an idol.

In the life, death, and resurrection of Jesus of Nazareth, we have a test for any power, or will, or desire, or decision that we might be tempted to attribute to God; and that means that we also have a test for any claim to power, will, desire, or decision on our own part – any power, will, desire, or decision that we might be tempted to justify as obedience to God. And so Williams can boldly reply to one critic of religion in the aftermath of September 11:

> faith becomes the one wholly inflexible ground for resistance to violence, precisely because it . . . allows us to recognize power for what it is and isn't: as what is given us for the setting-free of each other; not as the satisfying of our passion for control.[3]

Faith resists violence, because it tests our violent desires at the bench of Jesus' cross.

Williams distinguishes carefully between the model of 'obedience' which makes sense in Christian theology, and that which makes sense for a theology in which arbitrary power is uppermost. In the latter, groundless divine decrees may be obeyed or implemented, but they do not lead towards a 'hinterland' of divine nature to be contemplated or enjoyed. Groundless divine will does not propose to us anything of the elusive riches of God's life as such, to be regarded with eagerness or expectation of further fulfillment: the only 'mystery' is the sheerly negative awareness of the void from which divine enactment freely comes.[4]

In such a picture, if we ask 'Why should I do this?', God finally replies only 'Because I told you so,' and we are faced with an impenetrable wall behind which God's unknowable reasons reside. In a Christian understanding, however,

> God's voluntary actions are all, fundamentally, aspects of the diffusion and sharing of divine life, and our proper response is receptivity to this, discernment of that divine self-bestowal and enjoyment of it.[5]

Christian obedience is not blind acquiescence to the arbitrary dictates of an unpredictable deity, but precisely that journey deeper and deeper into the disarming love of God to which the Gospel calls us – that journey in eagerness and expectation deeper and deeper into contemplation and enjoyment of the disarming love which goes all the way down in God, that love which is the life of God.

II

Christians are called, according to Williams, to the ongoing task of working at all our ways of speaking about God in order to root out of them anything that has not been shaped by the Gospel. The God of the Gospel is one who loves; so Christian theology must learn to speak in such a way as to show that love in God goes all the way down, and is not trumped by power. The God of the Gospel is one who gives life; so Christian theology must find ways of proclaiming that God is wholly, unreservedly giving. The God of the Gospel is one who is not defeated by our betrayals and failures, but who always continues to call us to fellowship; Christian theology is called to think of God in ways which do not limit the resourcefulness of his call, the creativity of his love.

This far from abstract concern underlies a good deal of Williams' most fearsomely technical and detailed academic work – particularly some of his earliest work, on very involved aspects of Russian Orthodox philosophical theology,[6] and some of his detailed historical work on the Trinitarian debates of the fourth century. As he analyses it, for instance, the bishops who met at the Council of Nicaea in AD 325 – the council responsible for the first draft of what was to become our 'Nicene Creed' – clashed swords over precisely this question of the relationship between God's power and God's love. In the work of Arius, the Alexandrian presbyter condemned at Nicaea, Williams finds a theology so concerned to protect God's mysterious, unknowable transcendence and omnipotence that it requires us to imagine an inaccessible divine Holy of Holies lying behind all that we can know of God, confined as we are in the outer courts: a totally unknowable, unplumbable source from which all that we know of God – God as Father, God as loving, the God of the Gospel – is produced. The unknowable source itself, unlike that which it decides to produce for our benefit, cannot be characterized as Father, as involved, as loving: those are words that remain only and exclusively appropriate to the outer courts, not to the ineffable Holy of Holies; that dark divine 'hinterland' remains eternally pure, eternally unconnected, eternally unsullied by relationship with creatures.

For Nicene theology, on the other hand – at least as it eventually emerged from the debates that were to sputter and flare for decades after the Council – 'there is no overplus of "unengaged" and inexpressible reality, nothing that is not realized in and as relationship, in God'.[7] That is, there is nowhere we can go in God, no extra we can think about or point to, no reservation, no sanctuary, in which God is not engaged, involved, loving, and relational. God is love, all the way down. The supporters of the Nicene Creed insisted that being a Father – being one who brought forth, loved, and gave himself to a Son – was not, as it were, something which God decided at some point to enter into, not something which happened to a God whose nature was already defined apart from that relationship; it was not something which God decided to add to a portfolio of characteristics which was already coherent and complete. No: for Nicene theology God is always, eternally, Father and Son. That relationship is intrinsic to who God is, and there is nowhere in God that we can go which is defined apart from, or prior to, that relationship. God is not one who *decides* to give; God is eternally giving, eternally relating.

To think of God as anything like an isolated individual who *decides* to come into relationship is to betray the Gospel – it is to reserve some part or aspect of God's being from the Gospel, to say that there is some territory in God which is not thoroughly caught up in the Gospel. We have to think instead of God as something more like a community of persons relating to one another – as a rich *life* of relating, giving and receiving; a life that can be shared with us, a life into which we can be invited, without it having to change fundamentally in nature or have some new character bolted onto it. As Williams puts it,

> The whole notion of a God who is 'productive', free to create a world to which he can communicate something of himself, *depends upon* conceiving God's intrinsic life as generative of relation: the creation of the world only makes full theological sense in the light of a belief in the everlasting generation of the Son from the Father; the shape of the redeemed life is the realizing in our world of an eternal actuality.[8]

The only alternative is to believe that God, in relating to us, in sharing with us, in loving us, is doing something essentially *foreign* to his nature – that his nature is to be isolated, self-sufficient, unrelated, and that what we meet in this relating, sharing, and loving is therefore not the real God, not God as he most centrally is. No, says Williams; 'God gives eternally, necessarily, out of the very depth of His being.'[9] God is love, all the way down.

III

Jacob could not accept Esau's welcome without the suspicion that Esau was secretly pursuing his own interests – the suspicion that Esau was still, even in this welcome, a rival. The Gospel can only be heard as Gospel – can only be heard as liberating – if we hear it as acceptance by one who loves entirely without self-interest and rivalry; as a love which does not bend us to a foreign end. Christians believe that we have met such love in Jesus of Nazareth – and that we meet it in him because he is the act of God, because God's act of loving acceptance works through him unimpeded. Part of what is implied by the Gospel for our understanding of God is therefore the claim that God is not self-interested, that God does not have 'interests' in the normal sense at all. He doesn't have personal needs, tensions he feels the need to resolve, problems he has to work through using the world as his worry-beads.

For Williams, this sets a question mark against any way of picturing God which assumes – to put it crudely – that God has a psychology like ours, only bigger. He speaks of the Christian tradition's 'warning against canonizing in theology the tempting idioms of human personal interaction, requiring us to strain beyond these if we are to begin to hold to any sense of the radicality of divine gift'.[10] That is not to say that we need to move away from the language of 'life', of 'love', of 'relationship' – emphatically not that – but rather that we should be wary of relying too strongly on language about God which makes God's life any kind of *drama*, whether a psychological drama of pondering and deciding, tension and resolution, or a social drama of episodes and events among a set of characters.

Using a slightly different idiom, Williams can say that God is 'not an individual' (nor three individuals). He doesn't mean that it is inappropriate to describe God in personal terms; he is using the language in a more technical way, to insist that there are some important ways in which God is not like us:[11]

If God is not an individual, God does not compete with us

for space; if God is not an individual, God's will cannot be adequately understood in the terms of self-assertion or contest for control in which so much of our usual discourse of will is cast.[12]

The creeds are sometimes criticized for taking us away from a pure, simple belief in one God and towards a complex mythology of three interacting persons, and of journeys from heaven to earth and earth to heaven – a step in the direction of the messy myths of gods and men from which the austere lines of monotheism had saved us. For Williams, however, 'The creed of Nicaea is a first step in the critical *de*mythologising of Christian discourse'[13] – it takes us away (as I have been stressing) from even the refined, minimal mythology of a God who at some point, according to some inaccessible internal history, *decides* to relate; it is the first step in a Christian reflection which denies tension and resolution, sequence, drama and plot to God's internal life. It leaves us with, on the one hand, an eternal, unchanging divine life of threefold relation, and on the other an utterly creaturely, contingent, changing, finite, universe, itself completely dependent upon that divine life. History, drama, and contingency, the contest of wills, the meeting of needs, the resolving of tensions, characterize creation, not the Creator.[14] The only history that God has is the history of the Universe which he upholds – and with it, the history of Israel, the history of the Church, and above all the history of Jesus: *that* is God's history, and he has no other.

Williams does not, of course, deny that the Bible and the Christian tradition speak pervasively in terms which present God as an individual with interests, and with an internal history. And he acknowledges, too, that we can't avoid doing the same – and should not try too hard to avoid doing the same. He himself speaks, for instance, of God loving 'the reflection of his love within creation; he cannot bear to be separated from it and goes eagerly in search of it, hungry to find in the created "other" the reality of his own life and bliss'.[15] But he acknowledges that this language is not straightforward; it is 'extreme', it is 'bold', and as we reflect on it we need to interpret it carefully.[16] We have to speak in such bold terms; they are the only ones available to us, and the only ones which enable us to point to the nature of God's love with any adequacy. But we also have to recognize that the language is not wholly adequate: it points us towards, but does not enable us to grasp, the nature of God's love – which remains always wider and deeper than our understanding of it. The same Christian tradition that continues to use this bold, individual-ized language also teaches us the ways in which this language fails to capture its object – reminding us that its timeless, simple, unchanging object transcends drama and psychology.

Williams particularly stresses this necessary boldness of our language – and the necessity of undercutting it and recognizing its inadequacy – when it comes to God's *action*. Certainly the Bible and the tradition present us with many descriptions of God acting in particular ways in particular situations, in language that we can only normally make sense of by thinking in terms of an individual immersed in the situation, responding and making decisions on the go – in terms, that is, of an individual with a psychology and a history. Williams acknowledges that we inherit language like this, and that we too must use it – but once again he argues that the Christian tradition of reflection on the nature of God qualifies this language: it says, 'Yes, but . . .' Trying to sketch what it might mean to do justice to this language of par-ticular acts in particular places without undermining the sense that God is *not* an individual, that God does *not* have a history, Williams speaks instead of a single all-encompassing divine act which underlies and works through all that is, and then says:

> If there are moments when the act of God is recognised more plainly than it is in others, or when the subject senses a close-ness to the underlying act of God that has the effect of prompt-ing, warning, reassuring or guiding, we are not to think of the fabric of the finite order being interrupted, but rather of the world being such that, given certain configurations of finite agencies, the texture of the environment is more clearly trans-parent to the simple act of divine self-communication.[17]

This language about 'fabric', 'texture', 'transparency' is, of course, also pictorial language – language drawn from our world of time and things. No more than the language of a God with psychology and history does it give us a final, complete *grasp* of what we mean by talk of God 'acting'. But it acts as a vital qualification on that other language, reminding us that, although we can't avoid using such language and must take it seriously, it remains inadequate and we cannot allow all of its ordinary implications.

The discussion of this point can quickly become very technical, and feel like it is turning language about God into a curious game for philosophical experts. Nevertheless, we should remember that the driver behind it is, for Williams, still the Gospel. He moves in this direction in order to make full sense of God as one who does not compete with us, who does not jostle us for space. He wants to avoid any hint that God can be at work only in the *gaps* in our world, where other actors, other agencies, are pushed aside to make room for him. This picture will not do. If God's act is seen most clearly in the free human action of Jesus of Nazareth, then it is not seen where creaturely actions are being shouldered aside to make way for divine action – not, that is, where God is one actor among many – but rather where divine action is the deep, generative ground, the wellspring, the guiding source, of creaturely actions; the context in which they take place, the territory they explore. God is not one more character on the script, one with whom we must negotiate: he is the author of the script, the paper on which it is written.

For Williams, God is therefore the only one who can tell us who we are. Among all the competing claims which others make on us, seeking to dictate to us who we shall be, we discover our proper identities not by struggling for an entirely illusory independence but by turning to our deepest, purest dependence – the undistorting dependence of creatures on their Creator. If it makes sense for a child to wish eventually to become independent from her parents, to discover her own life beyond their control, it does not make the same kind of sense to imagine becoming mature enough to be independent of oxygen – to discover one's own life beyond one's cloying dependence on the air one breathes. Our dependence upon God is more like the latter than the former: because God has no agenda, no 'interests' in that sense, there can be no shadow of a suspicion that he is trimming us to fit neatly into the gaps in his life; God is no tender of bonsai trees, trimming and wiring until they match the shapes which he has in mind, his personal idea of beauty, regardless of the wilder, messier shape inherent in the trees themselves. When God becomes a concrete presence in our lives in Jesus of Nazareth, our conversation with him is not one more way in which we get shaped to fit some-body else's agenda: it is our route home, our gateway to discover-ing ourselves. God is the soil in which we grow. The activity by which we grow towards our true shape, the activity which is our purest freedom, *is* God's life flowing through us.

IV

We mistake the nature of speech about God if we think that it is a matter of sitting back and arriving at a neutral description of God from the comfort of our study chairs. Speech about God finds its place in a life which is being drawn into the life of God – in the process of our being remade by the Gospel of disarming acceptance. And, as such, our speech about God, our ideas about God, our theology, needs to share in the same characteristics that mark a life being captivated by the Gospel: thankfulness and openness to judgement. So, in the first place, we receive our lan-guage about God as a gift, and celebrate it; in the second place, we need constantly to be open to the breaking and remaking of our language, as the truth of the Gospel works upon our lives and our ideas.

Williams constantly stresses the necessity of this openness to judgement, and does so in part by speaking about the 'nega-tive way' or the 'apophatic' nature of theology – by which he simply means that on our journey ever deeper into God's love, our language and ideas do not escape the way of the cross. Draw-ing upon the Russian Orthodox theologian on whom he wrote his doctoral thesis, Williams says that the negative way is 'the metanoia [that is, the repentance] of the intellect' within 'the metanoia of the whole human person'.[18] It is the willingness to let go, to have our ideas stripped bare and remade; theology itself must be 'metanoia, even crucifixion'.[19]

> [F]aith is *always*, not only in this life, a longing and trust directed away from itself towards an object to which it will never be adequate, which it will never comprehend. God is what we have not yet understood, the sign of a strange and unpredictable future.[20]

There is always more of God; God is always breaking out of the conceptual boxes into which we have placed him. We cannot predict where the journey into knowledge of God's love will take us.

Williams finds something like this proclaimed in the resurrection, drawing a parallel between the stories of the empty tomb, and the stories of the empty space between the cherubim on the top of the ark of the covenant in the Old Testament. The latter functioned as a constant reminder to Israel that their God was no idol, that God could not be circumscribed, tied down, or decisively and finally located. It reminded them that their God was an uncontrollable and inexhaustible presence. The empty tomb, Williams suggests, does something similar for us: it prevents us from thinking that Jesus' identity and work is finished and receding into the past; it prevents us from thinking that we have done with it and can move on to new things or supposedly deeper levels of spirituality. The Jesus who is represented by the empty tomb is a Jesus who has a continued, uncontrollable, and inexhaustible presence;[21] the Jesus represented by the empty tomb cannot be controlled or tied down or finished with. '[T]he empty tomb tradition', Williams says, 'is, theologically speaking, part of the Church's resource in resisting the temptation to "absorb" Jesus into itself, and thus part of what its confession of the divinity of Jesus amounts to in spiritual and political practice.'[22] And if Jesus, our gateway to knowledge of God, resists this absorption, how much more does the God to whom he points? (Incidentally,

Williams asks whether this means that he must 'think belief in the empty tomb as an historical fact is essential to belief in the resurrection?' His answer is blunt: 'Actually, yes.'[23] He does not see how he can hold to the kind of Gospel he proclaims – a resurrection Gospel – unless he also holds firmly to the empty tomb.)

A more characteristic way in which Williams speaks about this theme is by referring to Christ's infancy. If Jesus' whole life is God's word to us, then he is God's word not only when he is intelligible, not only when he makes clear sense – not only when he is graspable and usable by us. He is also God's word when he is wrapped in swaddling clothes and laid in a manger. Williams notes our temptation to make the 'tightly swaddled baby' of the Christmas stories into 'a gift-wrapped object, passive and docile for use in *our* business, *our* transactions; a lucky mascot; the sleeping partner in the firm (the little Lord Jesus asleep on the hay)' – 'little Lord Jesus, like Little Lord Fauntleroy, who generates in us such good and warm feelings that we *know* we can't be wrong'.[24] Williams reminds us just how strange a view this is:

> 'The cattle are lowing, the baby awakes / But little Lord Jesus, no crying he makes.' Every parent in Christendom must have blinked with incredulous envy at this miracle: never mind the angels and the star, a baby who doesn't cry when surrounded by a herd of hungry cows is much more of a prodigy! Babies, in fact, may be wordless and dependent, but they are not as a rule silent, nor are they passive. They make their presence felt, they alter lives; their dependence is a matter of fingers clutching at ours when we'd like to be getting on with something; broken nights, hungry mouths at the breast; the need to be taught and watched and entertained, brought into the world of human speech and relation. If God is with us as a child – a *real* child – he is not after all so tidily gift-wrapped, so functional. If God is with us as a child, he is certainly with us as one who calls out our tenderness and compassion; but he does so by an insistent presence without shame or restraint, crying and clutching. He is the God who, in St. Augustine's unforgettable words, penetrates my deafness by his violent loud crying . . . So far

from the divine child being a cipher, the tool of our schemes and systems, he confronts us with the alarming, mysterious, shattering strangeness of God.[25]

That Jesus is also God's word to us when he is this child reminds us that God is not simply there to meet our needs, and that our language about and understanding of God – which tries to wrap him up, tie him down, and place him silent in the manger – needs interrupting, needs to be made aware of its deafness. We are too prone to relish the success of our language about God, to think that we have understood – that our smooth, neatly interlocking concepts allow us to grasp all that really needs to be said about God. Williams takes the disturbing, interrupting, uncontrollable nature of a child's crying as a sign of the wildly prolific, difficult, messy, uncontrollable, inelegant, disturbing nature of the language about God that we find in our Bible and in the testimonies of obstinate believers who refuse to see things in quite the way we do, and therefore as a sign of the ways in which God escapes all our language.

> [T]here is a terrible aptness, a rhetorical rightness, in a God who speaks in a child's cry. And it is so cruelly hard – for believer and unbeliever alike – to face the possibility that silence, stumbling apparent crudity, tell you more of God than the language of would-be adult sophistication. As if the best theology were the noise of someone falling over things in the dark.[26]

It is God himself who lobs rocks into the smooth pond of our language about God, shattering our complacency – and only so can he keep us from preferring the idols which our words construct. '[W]e must be surprised, ambushed and carried off by God,' Williams says, 'if we are to be kept from idols.'[27] 'God himself is the great "negative theologian", who shatters all our images by addressing us in the cross of Jesus.'[28]

When we think about God, there is always an extent to which we end up fitting him into our world, as one element in it among others. We simply can't think God's absolute difference from the world, and God's absolute intimacy to it; we can only gesture towards such an understanding with inadequate pictures and images. We need constantly to be reminded that the reality towards which even our best words gesture transcends them and exceeds them – that, however much they are appropriate ingredients in the process by which we are drawn into the life of God, and weaned from self-serving idols, all our words fail radically to grasp God. The God we can think, the God we fit into our mental schemas, the God we can put on a list of things we understand, is not God.[29] Williams traces how this is played out in the Gospel of Mark:

> Throughout the Gospel, Jesus holds back from revealing who he is because, it seems, he cannot believe that there are words that will tell the truth about him in the mouths of others . . . Whatever is said will take on the colouring of the world's insanity; it will be another bid for the world's power, another identification with the unaccountable tyrannies that decide how things shall be. Jesus, described in the words of this world, would be a competitor for space in it, part of its untruth.[30]

It is only when he is in a position where all the words we associate with God or with God's messiah obviously fail – only, that is, when he is on trial, stripped and bound, 'denuded of whatever power he might have had', on his way to the death his captors have chosen for him – only then that 'he speaks plainly about who he is'.

> Jesus breaks his silence at this moment in the trial because only now can what he says be heard. There is little or no danger that we shall now mistake what he means, that we shall confidently describe him in words that reflect our own aspirations. He is who he is, and we can do nothing but let our imagination and our language be reshaped by him – if, that is, we have ears to hear, if we are not already determined to abide by the standards of the insane world that has brought him to trial.[31]

If, that is, we have ears to hear: the temptation when reading this is to think that this warning applies to other people, to people who have not heard the Gospel, perhaps, or people who perversely cling to a theology less pure than ours. *They* are the ones who need to hear this; *we*, of course, have ears to hear . . . No doubt the High Priest and his court, who knew their Scriptures well and prayed and worshipped often, would have said something similar. Yet for us, as for them, to defend ourselves in this way from Jesus' challenge is already for our voices to slip into the old accents of 'the insane world'; it is to close our ears to God's shattering judgement.

The process of being given ears to hear, of being weaned from the world's insanity (*our* insanity) is long and painful; it is the process by which we are stripped of our selfishness and polished into mirrors for the love of God. We may relax and rest content with the current state of our language about God, the concepts with which we describe him, at exactly the same moment that we may relax and rest content with the state of our sanctification. And that moment may be a while coming.

> We are not . . . permitted to be at home in the sense that we can feel ultimately satisfied with where and what we are, longing to hold on to it and unwilling to respond to challenge; we are not to settle down in our place and our time because we feel comfortable. There are always questions to be asked by us and of us.[32]

Should we, then, throw up our hands and admit that we know nothing of God – that all our words fail radically, so that any words will do, and no words would be better? To say that would be to take back the claims with which we began this chapter – to turn back to an idea of radical divine indeterminacy, a great well of darkness beneath the surface of God's love, unplumbed by what we say or know of that love. This is not – absolutely not – Williams' point. This restless journey into God, with its attendant breaking and remaking of all our images, is a journey into God's love, a journey into God's life, a journey into all that is opened to us in Jesus of Nazareth. In Christian theology,

Williams says, 'The unknowability of God ceases to be simply the inaccessibility of a kind of divine "hinterland", the mysteriousness of an indefinite source of divinity.' The unknowability of God is not the unknowability of an object too far away for us to make out; it is the unknowability of one who is too close, too all-encompassing, for us to hold at arm's length. As Williams stresses at every available opportunity, there is nothing in God that is kept back from relationship, from gift, from involvement.

> [T]he divine nature cannot be abstracted from God's active relationship with the world. And since that relationship, in which the theologian as believer is caught up, is not susceptible of being distanced and exhaustively defined, neither is God's nature. His everlasting act is as little capable of being a determinate object to our minds as the wind in our faces and lungs can be held still and distant in front of our eyes.[33]

The negative way, the way of the cross, along which all our ideas and images and words prove inadequate, is not a journey into randomness and dissolution; it is 'a ceaseless growing into what is always and already greater and does not itself either grow or diminish', into 'the fullness of the divine'; it is 'a steady and endless enlarging of the heart'.[34]

V

The Gospel calls us to journey ever deeper into the divine life. It calls us to journey ever deeper into God's acceptance of us, ever deeper into God's disarming of our selfishness, ever deeper into the knowledge that all around us are also loved by God. It is a journey in which we more and more become reflections of God's selfless love.[35] It is not a journey to the kind of knowledge of God which can aptly be thought of as me standing over against an object and getting a clear view of it, inspecting and mastering it. It is rather a journey into a life in which I am more and more mastered by the reality I am exploring. It is, perhaps, a journey into the kind of knowledge one has when one learns to play or sing a piece of music – where it becomes possible to say, 'You are the music while the music lasts.' [36] The reality of the music takes one over, not in violent overthrow or colonization, but in and through one's own action, one's own dedication to it. This is a kind of knowledge where the relationship between knowing subject and known object is not one of distant but accurate inspection; rather it is the kind of knowledge one has when 'What is *happening* in the subject . . . is what the object is doing, the way in which it is making itself present to the subject.' Williams draws on the language used in Eastern Orthodoxy to describe this as 'the deification of man in grace' – not meaning that a person loses his or her finite, mortal creatureliness in this process, but that a person can long for 'the identification of his *will* with God's: what he effects is what God effects, his acts are, as it were, God's, while still remaining his'.[37] Williams speaks of a longing for a kind of union with God, in which 'the self is *surrendered* at a radical level to the activity of God, so that it can no longer be thought of as acting from a centre separated from God'.[38]

The idiom of 'deification' and of 'union' may be unfamiliar, but the same vision can be put in more prosaic words:

> God's pure, causeless, gratuitous love can have no answer, except some faint fumbling echo of that very gratuity and pointlessness itself . . . It is only when we learn to give, not from a sense of debt but from an overflowing joy, that we can have some share in the action of his redeeming and recreating love.[39]

The end towards which we are travelling is not the ability accurately to describe an object held at arm's length, but the strengthening of that 'faint, fumbling echo', so that our whole lives become sounding boards for it – every nerve and muscle fibre vibrating to this sound, so that there is nothing in us that does not play out God's music in the world.

There is another way of putting all this – and it is, for Williams, the key to understanding it properly. The goal towards which we are being drawn is to 'stand where Jesus stands as Christian believers, and pray as Jesus prays; and in standing in that place before God as "Abba" [to] share equally in Jesus' directedness towards the good and the healing of the world'.[40] The discipleship to which we are called is discipleship to Jesus of Nazareth; the music to which we are called to vibrate is the theme played out without distortion in his life, death, and resurrection. He is the original transcription of that divine, eternal music into a form playable on finite, human instruments, and it is only because we hear that music transcribed in him that we can take it up ourselves – or be taken up by it ourselves. Our journey is a journey towards standing where Christ stands; the life of discipleship is a journey with the Son, to the Father.

With the Son, *to* the Father – and *in* the Holy Spirit. We have finally reached the point where we are in a position to understand Williams' discussion of the doctrine of the Trinity. He asks us, by way of introduction, to consider what it means to say that we are called to stand where Christ stands, to *share* in his relationship to the Father. If we picture the love between Father and Son as like that found between two young lovers, it would be hard to know what could be meant by *sharing* in it, by standing alongside one of the lovers and participating in his relationship with his partner. That is, we can't understand sharing in a love which is entirely absorbed by the particular face of the one loved; the kind of love which is *exhausted* by the particular relationship in which it flares up, so that there is no space for anyone else. (And many of us will have had the experience of being awkwardly present with two young lovers, and feeling like an intruder, an unwanted extra – a 'gooseberry'.) If the love between Father and Son is a love in which we can participate, a love which we can share, then it must differ from this. There must be an *openness* to it; it cannot be *exhausted* by the particular identities of Father and Son: there must be, as Williams puts it, an 'excess' to it,[41] a 'capacity' into which we can be drawn. And this, Williams says, is the Spirit: the Spirit is God's 'infinite capacity for "new" activity, new and yet constant, faithful to His purpose'; God's infinite capacity for including new members in his life.[42]

We have already said that the relationship of Jesus of Nazareth to the one he calls Father is the transcription into the world of history of an eternal relationship within God, for God is eternally Father and Son. The Incarnation is the opening out of this relationship so that we can see it – and so that we can be drawn into it. What Williams now stresses is that, if we take seriously the idea that we are to be drawn into this relationship between Father and Son, rather than simply contemplating it from a distance, this picture of God as eternally Father and Son is inadequate on its own. The power of the Spirit that we experience shaping us, drawing us into the Son's relationship to the Father – the 'excess', the 'openness', the 'generativity' of this relationship between Jesus and the one he calls Father – is the transcription into our world of a similar 'excess' in the eternal relationship between Father and Son, an *eternal* openness in that relationship. We cannot think of the relationship between Father and Son in eternity as being the kind of relationship entirely exhausted by each of them absorbed in the particularity of the other, but must think of it as involving something *more* – and that more is not an impersonal attribute, not a passive characteristic, but is an active openness in the life of God, an active giving *of* the life of God, by God.[43] Williams argues that we have to think of this active giving as a third 'person' – a third distinct reality – in the eternal relational life which is God.[44] We have to think of God as Father, Son, and Holy Spirit – as Trinity.

This may sound fearsomely technical. The crucial point, however, can be put in fairly simple, fairly accessible ways, which make clear how close it is to the ordinary stuff of Christian life. We may point, for instance, to the experience of Christian prayer as prayer in the Spirit, with the Son, to the Father. Christian prayer is not, that is, to be pictured simply as 'us down here' praying to 'God up there'; rather it is us praying alongside Christ who prays truly to the Father; it is us praying in the power of the Spirit who prays truly in us and through us, animating our prayers, and drawing them into Christ's prayer. It is no less God who animates our prayers, no less God into whose prayer we are included, than it is God to whom we pray. In prayer, we are caught up in a threefold relational life – caught up by the Spirit into the Son's relationship to the Father.

So, however difficult the technical arguments may become, the discussion always remains tied to the reality of our inclusion – the inclusion of diverse multitudes of human beings – in the love of Son and Father. In this vision, the Spirit is the one who 'interprets . . . the relation of Father and Son; and he interprets it by re-creating, *translating* it, in the medium of human existence'. 'The Spirit's witness is . . . the formation of "Son-like" life in the human world.'[45] And to talk about the reality of this interpretation, this formation, is not the same as talking about either Father or Son:

> The grammar of our talk about the Holy Spirit is not that proper to 'God' as source, ground, terminus of vision and prayer, and so forth, nor that proper to 'God' as the disturbing presence of grace and vulnerability within the world of human relationships as a particular focal story. It is the grammar of 'spirituality' in the fullest sense of that emasculated word.[46]

That is, when we speak about God's Spirit, we are speaking about the refraction of the pure light of God's disturbing grace and vulnerability into the rainbow of diverse human lives – the full, rich orchestration of the theme played simply in Jesus, by the formation over time of billions of diverse Son-like, Father-directed lives. With the same boldness with which Paul can speak, in Colossians 1.24, of us 'completing what was lacking in Christ's afflictions', Williams says that

> the actual concrete meaning of logos in the world, the pattern decisively and transformingly embodied in Jesus, could *only be seen and realized* through the entire process of the history to which the event of Jesus gives rise, with all its fluidity and unpredictability.[47]

> [H]uman history is the story of the discovery or realization of Jesus Christ in the faces of all women and men. The fullness of Christ is always *to be* discovered.[48]

Exploration of the nature of God, then, is not a matter of working towards accurate verbal descriptions of God, but nor is it simply a matter of individuals finding the quality of love growing within them; rather, it is seen most fully in the growth of a world-wide community being drawn together, in all its diversity, into discipleship, struggling to find a form of life together appropriate to the reality into which they are all being drawn, and struggling to do justice to the unlimited love of the Father, the disruptive presence in our world of the Son, and the diverse, untameable work of the Spirit within and beyond them.

VI

There is, in all this, a vision of the world as something like a chandelier: God's light at the centre of all things streams out, and is caught and refracted in thousands upon thousands of crystals, created to reflect the central light to one another and back to him. Crystals may be fractured or smeared, but the light is fierce enough to burn them clean, and to melt them enough to heal their wounds. Or perhaps the vision is closer to plumbing than to lighting: God's life is a great river, and we are channels – more or less clogged, all too often sitting across the main flow; the river however is strong enough to turn us around and clean us out – to allow us to do the job for which we were created, passing on this stream to others. Whatever metaphors one chooses, however, there is something overwhelming at work: a searing light or a torrential current; a life that refuses to be domesticated. Just as with his focus upon the cross, Williams' vision of God will allow us no easy Gospel: to know God is to be caught in this fierce current, and to have all the comforting accretions which have cushioned us against its flow stripped away, one by one.

If the Church is to do justice to a vision like this, then we must realize more clearly than we sometimes do that our journey into knowledge of God is an unending, and sometimes a painful journey, on which our images of God need repeatedly to be torn down and remade – and that our sacraments and liturgies, our hymns and songs, our sermons, our courses and retreats, all exist to serve this journey. And it may be that one of the gifts which Williams has to bring to the Church is a renewed sense of this never-ending journey of discovery – a renewed sense of our calling to throw ourselves into this current, without reserve – a renewed sense of the Church as a place of lifelong learning, for God's sake.

Chapter Three

Cloud of Witnesses

I

The Gospel involves us in processes of learning. In the first place, the Gospel is not a message that we can tell ourselves – it is not the sort of message that can be derived from a little introspection or analysis: we need to hear it, to be won into it – to be taught it. And its implications are not immediately and totally transparent: we need time and we need help if we are to learn to walk in its light. One of the characteristics of Williams' theology is his insistence on passing from discussion of the conceptual structure of the Gospel, or discussions of the nature of the God who encounters us in the Gospel, to discussion of how it is that we *learn* these things in the midst of the world. In this chapter, we will be looking at several aspects of this learning: how it is that we are taught the Gospel in Scripture; how it is that this scriptural Gospel is explored in the Christian tradition and in doctrine; how it is that the Church which lives that tradition points us toward and involves us in the Gospel – and how, in particular, the Eucharist is a school in which we learn this Gospel.

The Gospel calls us to 'steady and radical exposure to the fundamental events of Christian faith',[1] steady and radical exposure to God's love made visible in Jesus of Nazareth and in the history of which he was a part. The Gospel, because it is not simply *illustrated* by what took place in Jesus of Nazareth, but rather *constituted* by that history, cannot ever dispense with reference to him. It therefore involves an inescapable paying of attention to a reality which is not simply ready to hand, or easily within our grasp:

it involves hearing things we could not know unless we were told them. Theology, therefore, relies utterly upon witnesses to the life, death and resurrection of Jesus of Nazareth, and there- fore 'will necessarily accord central and decisive importance to Scripture, since Scripture is the unique witness to those events'.[2] Theology, if it is to speak about the Gospel, has to be scriptural – in the sense that it must be, by means of Scripture, exposed to God's unsettling love as it showed itself in one particular history; it must be tripped up by it, turned round by it, questioned by it, and provoked to wonder by it. In fact, 'The essential test of a theology claiming to be "scriptural",' according to Williams, 'is whether it begins and ends in this sort of *wonder*.'[3]

Williams is unapologetic about the scriptural basis of theo- logy, and can be very forthright about what it is that we learn from this witness, this 'unique touchstone of truth about God'. 'I believe that the Bible tells us what we could not otherwise know', he says:

> it tells us that God, the maker of the world, is committed to that world and desires with all his being to save it from disas- ter and the imprisonment of sin; that he does this by calling a people to witness to him by their prayers and their actions, in obedience to what he shows them of his will through the Law; that he brings this work to completion when God the eternal Son, the eternal Word, becomes human as Jesus of Nazareth and offers his life to destroy or to 'soak up', as you might say, the terrible consequences of our sin; and that Jesus is raised from the tomb to call a new people together in the power of the Spirit, who will show what kind of God God is in the quality of their life together and their relation with him . . . This is the world of the Bible into which the Church has to be brought again and again.[4]

Williams suggests, though, that we have developed many ways of avoiding Scripture – many ways of refusing to listen to it, ways of refusing to pay attention to the witness it provides to some- thing intractably historical. There are obvious and overt ways in which this takes place, but there are also more subtle ways: Williams argues, for instance, that all too often we rush to substitute our unifying, systematizing, harmonizing readings or summaries of the text for the text itself – stepping away from the kind of historical *learning* to which this Gospel calls us, to something quicker, easier and more controllable. If we are not to run from Scripture, we need to pay attention to its rough, complicated, various, difficult surface; we need to resist premature claims to find unities and harmonies, testing all such claims against the intractable awkwardness of the text. Scripture's witness to Jesus of Nazareth is not the sort of thing that can be grasped all at once in an illuminating experience, but rather requires time taken in reading, re-reading, questioning and discussing.[5]

This, Williams suggests, is the core of *literal* reading. Non-literal reading is precisely that kind of reading which finds some technique for moulding the rough surface of the text into smooth contours that we can easily grasp and use. The literal reader, on the other hand, allows her purposes and plans to be derailed by the text; allows that it does not say exactly what she wants it to say – that it does not immediately and transparently translate without remainder into simple ideas that we can learn once and for all, and carry around in our heads. Rather, literal reading involves, fundamentally, *taking time* with the text; it involves the patience that avoids the rush to useful meaning, and keeps on coming back and back to the text, in the knowledge that it says more than we expect, and says it in ways that do not match what we expect. Literal reading involves us in a discipline of humility, finding ways of allowing ourselves to pay attention to the text's intractable resistance.

Literal reading takes time with the texts because it acknowledges that these texts take time to unfold their meanings. They are not, that is, the sort of texts that can be taken in at a glance or a series of glances – a series of useful bullet points and slogans, laid out ready for us to pick up and use. Rather, biblical texts tell stories, or build complex arguments, they comment upon earlier texts, they are qualified or illuminated by later texts, they take away with the right hand what they have just given with the left.

Think, for instance, of the strange fact that the New Testament preserves four Gospels. The reader concerned to rush to a harmonious or unified reading will need to *explain* away the differences, the particularities, of each Gospel – or at least reduce them to minor and clearly harmonious variations. The literal reader, on the other hand, will spend time with each Gospel, registering the differences between the portraits that each paints – the differences of style, of emphasis, of purpose, of interpretation. Rather than producing a harmony in which all differences are quickly resolved, the literal reader will know that these differing texts 'must be constantly re-read in counterpoint with each other'. The texts must be allowed to trip up our harmonies. 'There is no resting-place among or between the gospels,' Williams says; they 'oblige us to take time not only in the reading of one sequence but in the "cross-referenced" reading' that acknowledges their diversity.[6]

Literal reading will take time with the text because it recognizes that this text does not give its meanings immediately, but only over time, through the difficult interactions and mutual qualification of its parts. And the text gives its meanings in this way in part because it bears the marks of having been written over time – not, that is, by a single author setting down in one go a coherent vision, but by individuals and communities stretched over time, struggling to come to terms with the reality that they had encountered – and struggling to come to terms with one another. This text bears the marks, that is, of individuals and communities learning the Gospel in history. So a literal reading will also be one which pays attention to the historical nature of texts – to the fact that they are produced in history by historical beings, writing from particular points of view, and responding to and arguing with other points of view. Scripture was not, after all, dropped fully formed from heaven.

And that means that we read the Scriptures as texts written by men and women like us, gathered by the Spirit into enlivening, crucifying encounter with God. They were written by precarious, finite, weak and mortal people, who witness to the disarming acceptance of God precisely as they are shaped by it – as they are drawn closer to God, as their defensiveness and violence are stripped away, and as they learn what it means to live this Gospel.

> [T]he revelation of God comes to us in the middle of weakness and fallibility. We read neither with a kind of blind and thoughtless obedience to every word of scripture, as if it simply represented the mind of God, nor do we read with that rather priggish sensibility that desires to look down on the authors of scripture as benighted savages. We read with a sense of our own benighted savagery in receiving God's gift, and our solidarity with those writers of scripture caught up in the blazing fire of God's gift who yet struggle with it, misapprehend it, and misread it.[7]

We read as those who share in the same movement in which the biblical authors are caught up, drawn by the Spirit towards the Father.

Jesus of Nazareth is central to that movement. He is the one in whom that movement is unimpeded, and he acts therefore as the criterion for our judgements concerning where that movement is to be found. If Christ is the touchstone for the movement in which we and the biblical authors are caught up, then he is the touchstone for the Bible as well. It witnesses to a movement which finds its definitive form in him, and so a Christian reading of Scripture – a reading which looks to it as inspired revelation – will be a reading 'around Christ',[8] a reading in which we bring all the meaning that we think we are finding to the cross, to be judged and sifted there.

Williams accepts that there are times when this can mean that the witness which some portion of Scripture gives to this movement towards God, to God's drawing of us to himself, is oblique. To pick an example which, as far as I am aware, Williams does not discuss, we might ask what we are to do with the verse in Psalm 137 in which one of the exiles in Babylon calls down curses upon his captors: 'Happy shall they be who take your little ones and dash them against the rock.' Williams' suggestion, I think, would not be that we should simply cut this verse out of the Bible – but neither would it be that our job is to find some sense in which this sentiment is *acceptable*. (And, whether they acknowledge it or not, most Christian readers have had ways of suggesting that this isn't a text we can use in any straightforward way now.) If we allow our reading of this verse to be questioned and judged at the foot of the cross, we will have to refuse the violent fantasy which it offers to us. I think Williams would suggest, though, that we still need to take this verse seriously – to take seriously, perhaps, what it reveals about the cycle of violence and counter-violence in which we are caught, and about the dangerous liaisons which faith can enter into with that violence. In other words, we may find that, read in the stark light of the Gospel, this text offers an uncomfortable insight into our own 'benighted savagery'. Even a dark text like this has, in the light of the Gospel, a vital back-handed witness to give. We might say that such a text *becomes* Scripture precisely as it is allowed to give this witness in Jesus' light. 'When we approach the Bible,' Williams says, 'we must approach it as if it were . . . held open before us by the living Christ.'[9]

Williams does discuss a similar example, from the book of Revelation. In one of the letters to the churches which begin that book, we find a stark prophecy against 'that woman Jezebel' – including the threat that God 'will strike her children dead' (Rev. 2.23). 'We aren't called', Williams says, 'to believe and endorse' this passage – we aren't, that is, called to find some sense in which this curse is *acceptable*. We are, however, called to take this text seriously, and listen to it in the light of the Gospel; we are called, perhaps, 'to ask ourselves what we are taught here about the strangeness and sometimes the terror of the Word of God to fragile minds', recognizing that we may be just as fragile.[10] This is not a case of cutting out of the Bible those bits that we do not like, nor of reinterpreting it to suit the latest moral fashions. It is, rather, an attempt to be serious about the Bible as inspired revelation – about the Bible as produced by those caught up by the Spirit in movement towards the Father; it is an attempt to take seriously the positive witness of the Bible to that movement, but also to understand that, precisely as caught up in that movement, it too must stand under the judgement of the cross of Christ. Reading the Bible, too, we must resolve 'to know nothing but Christ and him crucified' (1 Cor. 2.2).[11]

> The Bible is not a human record from the distant past, full of a mixture of inspiring and not-so-inspiring stories or thoughts; nor is it a sort of magical oracle, dictated by God. It is rather the utterances and records of human beings who have been employed by God to witness to his action in the world, now given to us by God so that we may learn who he is and what he does; and the 'giving' by God is by means of the resurrection of Jesus. The risen Jesus takes hold of the history of God's people from its remotest beginnings, lifts it out of death by bringing it to completeness, and presents it to us as his word, his communication to us here and now.[12]

Williams' is a theology, then, that requires of us slow, patient, loving, repeated reading of Scripture; reading practised intensely and devoutly over years; reflective and prayerful reading; reading which begins and ends at the foot of the cross, however strange and difficult the journeys are which it takes along the way. But Williams' theology also requires us to read *in company*.[13] Because the Bible is not immediately and effortlessly transparent – because we do not simply open its pages and let its meanings leap fully formed into our minds – we constantly need to learn how to read from others, and to have our efforts at reading challenged by others. To accept the primacy of the difficult and awkward text, rather than the authority of my own smooth harmonization of it, means accepting the necessity and value of discussion, debate, argument, even conflict, between readers of the Bible. In the company of others, our reading can become richer, more nuanced, more alert to possibilities and connections that we would have overlooked on our own; it can become more aware of the leaps it is taking, the impositions it is unwittingly forcing onto the text, the background beliefs that it is taking for granted; it can be re-awoken to texts that have become too familiar. To read the Bible deeply and richly, we might say, requires the Church – requires a community of readers spread around the world and spread through the centuries, engaged in a long, argumentative, passionate exploration of what these texts have to offer. And it requires those marginal and foreign readings, readings from outside the Church, which read the text at an angle to the ways in which we are used to reading it, and so open our eyes to more of what is there, more of its potential and its difficulty: there is, potentially, no-one who cannot be used by God to teach us to be better readers of Scripture.[14] .

II

Thinking about how it is that the Scriptures help us to learn the Gospel leads us inevitably, then, into considering how the Church helps us to learn, because one way of seeing the Church is to see it as an ongoing community of readers, argumentative and unmanageable, but therefore a community which can give us the gift of a deeper reading of Scripture. The Christian tradition, in other words, can be thought of as a vast living exegesis of the Bible – a vast training ground in scriptural reading, a vast ongoing excavation of the riches which are buried there. We might put this more broadly, and say that the Church is the community of those being caught up together by the Spirit into the life of Christ before the Father – the community of those being formed around Christ, of those being made into reflections of Christ to one another. The Church is a vast, argumentative and unmanageable collection of readings of *Christ*: a vast collection of refractions of the light of Christ into the rainbow of billions of diverse faces, each of which helps us by the particular partial light that it reflects to see more of the glory of God in the face of Christ. The Church exists to teach us Christ. And it does this not primarily by being a collection of ways of talking *about* Christ; it is not as if the Church were simply a collection of theologians, each of whom had an opinion about the implications of the Gospel – but by being a collection of people caught up each in his or her own way in Christ's life.

The Church is the humanity Christ has made possible; its real history is the history of particular persons realizing by the Spirit's gift the new potential for human nature once it has been touched by divine agency, divine freedom, in Christ. At its heart is nothing else, nothing less than Christ's reality, and thus Christ's action – the ceaseless movement towards the Father that is the life of the eternal Son, responding to the out-flowing of the Father's life which generates it. That trinitarian pulse is the heartbeat of the Church.[15]

If the reality which the Church helps us to explore – the reality which it teaches – is that 'ceaseless movement towards the Father', then we need to be cautious about how we express the nature of the Church's teaching. It is not going to be simply the doling out of well-understood truths – a case of those who have reached and understood the truth handing out that truth to others. Rather the Church will teach by inviting others to join with it in learning, and by pointing them to the sources from which it itself is slowly learning.

If we had to choose between a Church tolerably confident of what it has to say and seeking only for effective means of saying it, and a Church constantly engaged in an internal dialogue and critique of itself, an exploration to discover what is central to its being, I should say that it is the latter which is the more authentic.[16]

Rather than thinking of the Church as the bearer of *answers*, it might be better to think about the Church as the bearer of a question – the bearer of the question which the Gospel poses; we might say with Williams that the Church is '[t]hat which transmits God's question from generation to generation'.[17] The Church teaches by pointing away from itself to the transforming, upsetting impact of Jesus – pointing not so much to a stable, achieved religious system as to a disruption which can bring all systems of religious practice and knowledge face to face with a reality that cannot be exhausted by any system. The Church's paradoxical task is to preserve this questioning – to find concrete forms of life, stable practices, and a learnable language that will keep alive the possibility of our hearing this disruption, and which will allow it to be felt far deeper and far wider than the circle of its original impact.[18]

Putting this another way, Williams can say that 'The Christian is involved in seeking conversion – the bringing to judgement of contemporary struggles, and the appropriation of some new dimension of the transforming summons of Christ in his or her own life';[19] the Christian, that is, is one who seeks to hear Christ's question ever more deeply in his or her own life, and seeks to bring others to hear that question too. The Christian's vocation is not to answer every question and make everything simple, but to bring every answer to Christ, to be questioned by him – and thereby, in a sense, to make everything difficult.

We do need to be careful not to speak about the Church 'bearing a question' in such a way as to suggest that its message has no *content* – as if it simply communicated the purely negative quality of 'disturbance' or 'disruptiveness', like a career heckler who will rail at anything any speaker has to say. To think that this is what Williams wants would, as the previous chapter should have made clear, be fundamentally to mistake his doctrine of God – to substitute a God of wild and groundless indeterminacy for the infinitely explorable depth and riches of God's gratuitous love. The Church does communicate a 'content', because it does believe it knows where the source of this questioning is, and does believe it knows the character of this questioning to be life-giving love.

And so Williams can on occasion speak of the Church's vocation in terms which sound less austere. 'The Church', he says,

> is essentially missionary in nature, seeking to transform the human world by communicating to it in word and act a truthfulness that exposes the deepest human fears and evasions and makes possible the kind of human existence that can pass beyond these fears to a new liberty. The Church, in claiming to exist for the sake of opening the world to the fuller life

in which God can be discerned as the controlling meaning of things, claims to have something to contribute to all human cultures, all human essays in the construction of meaning.[20]

Nevertheless, Williams' language is more often designed to alert us to the danger of seeing the Church as a bearer of a finished and complete righteousness, which it simply seeks to spread to others. The Church's learning, he insists, is fallible – often disastrously so. It would quickly become obvious and dangerous nonsense if we were to claim that the Church was the community which had *achieved* the fullness of the humanity which Christ has made possible. The Church is made up of those caught up in an enlivening, crucifying movement, and can only point from the ambiguous midst of that movement towards that movement's goal. '[T]he Church', Williams insists, 'is *never* the object of its own faith: it is necessarily under the judgement of what it points to.'[21] Just as a commentary on a text can only perform its function to the extent that it points one back to the text on which it is commenting, if it leads one deeper into that text, and if it acknowledges the text as the criterion by which it stands or falls, so Christian lives can only be 'readings of Christ', can only speak the truth, to the extent that they point away from themselves towards that which has caught them up, that which is transforming them. This pointing away takes place when, in worship, the worshipper stands back so that the one worshipped might appear; it takes place when, in thankfulness, any achievement or possession that the worshipper might have is re-read as a gift; and it takes place when, in self-criticism and in repentance, worshippers accept that they stand under the judgement of a reality which they do not control. '[W]e have no authoritative holiness of our own, we have no option but to admit the charge. We *are* impostors, travelling in borrowed clothes, under an assumed name, the name of Jesus.'[22] The Church exists as a witness to Christ, and only as a witness to Christ.

III

The Church, in order to *be* the Church, must constantly remind itself that it relies upon Christ, and that it can never substitute itself for Christ. It must constantly represent to itself the fact that *its* life rests upon *his* life. One of the central ways in which it does this is by preserving, at the heart of its ongoing practices, rites in which the nature of its life, and the nature of its relation to Christ's life, is spelt out – rites which we call sacraments. '[A] Christian community involved in activities it calls "sacramental" is a community *describing* itself in a way that is importantly at odds with other sorts of description,'[23] a community describing itself as caught up in exhilarating, crucifying movement towards God. In the Eucharist in particular, the Church 'shows itself its source and its criterion',[24] and the Eucharist is one abiding way in which the Church represents to itself the true nature of its own life, and so crystallizes the question that it has been given to pose to the world.

The Eucharist, then, is an action of the Church in which it reminds itself that it is dependent upon the prior action of Jesus of Nazareth. During his ministry, and climactically at the last supper, Jesus used food and drink as a vehicle for creating unexpected fellowship. He ate and drank with others – with sinners, with tax-collectors, even with Pharisees – without setting preconditions, sharing himself with them, welcoming them to share his life. When, at the last supper, Jesus broke and shared bread, and distributed wine, it was the climax of this strand of his ministry. He was once again establishing fellowship with his disciples without setting conditions upon that fellowship, sharing with both the faithful and the faithless; handing himself over to his disciples, rather than holding aloof and protecting himself from them. In the drama of that night, he was later to hand himself over more directly, by refusing to defend himself from his faithless disciples – and at the supper he already symbolically put passive bread and wine into their hands and declared that in handling it, the disciples were handling him, that they had power to do as they would with the life which he had gratuitously shared with them. He

> binds himself to vulnerability before he is bound (literally) by human violence. Thus, those who are at table with him, who include those who will betray, desert and repudiate him, are, if you like, frustrated as betrayers, their job is done for them by their victim . . . [He] makes the betrayers his guests and debtors, making with them the promise of divine fidelity, the covenant, that cannot be negated by their unfaithfulness.[25]

Within hours, he has died a bloody death on the cross, and his symbolic handing of his body and blood to the disciples at the supper has taken on deeper and more terrifying resonances. It was not simply a gift of his 'life' in some metaphorical sense which he placed in their hands; it was his physical life – his real body and blood. He was given into their hands for them to do with as they wished, and they betrayed and abandoned him, letting that body be broken and that blood spilt. The bread and wine of the supper become vehicles, now, not just of the life of fellowship which he has been sharing with others, but of his total, costly self-gift made upon the cross. And the last supper, as it were, 'reads' the cross *as* a gift – not as the unwilling tearing of Jesus' life from him, but as a gift freely made.

When we celebrate the Eucharist, then, after the cross, and after the resurrection, we relinquish the bread and wine as our possessions, matter under our control, and receive them back from Jesus' hands.[26] To receive bread and wine from his hands is to allow him to welcome us to his table; it is to accept the gift of fellowship, the sharing of his life, and it is to accept the gift which he made of his body and blood, as a gift made for us also: '[T]he great mark of discipleship to the risen Christ is, as the New Testament has it, that we eat and drink with him after his resurrection.'[27] This is a gift which sets no preconditions. It is given to faithful and faithless alike, and is given again and again despite the deepest failures and betrayals – and so it is a gift that demands everything of us.

This gift was, of course, first of all a gift given to specific disciples in a specific time and place, but Jesus' relationship to the Father allows us to understand it as a gift given in and through him by the Father of all, and the resurrection allows us to understand it as a gift which we can now receive from his hand wherever and whenever we are; for 'when the crucified Son is raised from the dead, we understand that the sacrifice lived by Jesus and consummated in the cross is an abiding reality, an indestructible life and an inexhaustible gift'.[28] This is no longer a giving confined to one table at a time. Williams accordingly sets his understanding of Christ's action in the Eucharist within an understanding of Christ's risen life:

> The glorified Christ, crucified and risen, is eternally active towards God the Father on our behalf, drawing us into the eternal movement of self-giving love that the Son or Word directs towards the source of all, the God Jesus calls 'Abba'. The sacrifice of the cross is, among other things, the 'transcription' into this world's terms of the Son's movement of love towards the Father in heaven. In the Eucharist, our prayer is swept into that current, and we are set free to share in the Son's self-giving. The giving of thanks over the elements renews for us the covenant made by God in Christ, and the work of God in the cross is again 'applied' to us, in word and action, in body and soul.[29]

The Eucharist is, in a sense then, the presence of Christ among us – but

> the presence that is appropriate and intelligible in the Eucharist is neither the presence of an idea in our minds . . . nor the presence of a uniquely sacred *object* on the Table. It is the presence of an active Christ, moving in love not only towards the Father but towards us.[30]

To celebrate the Eucharist, therefore, is to point back towards Christ's action: his action upon the cross, and his action as risen

Lord – and it is not to declare ourselves a perfect community, but rather to acknowledge ourselves a community held together despite our failures and betrayals by the capacious, gracious giving of Christ – a community given the terrifying privilege of handling this gift, and passing it on, made by this gift into givers. So the Eucharist is an activity of the Church in which the Church tells itself about the nature of its own life. It represents its life to itself: representing its life as a gift, representing itself as frail and fallible recipient of that gift, and representing itself as charged to carry that gift in the world – bearing the question of Christ wherever it might go.

IV

The process by which the Church 'bears the question' of the Gospel into new areas is one in which it continues to learn. Stepping into new locations, it is given new angles from which to see its own message, so that it is itself 're-converted' in the process of mission.[31] This is a process in which we learn the riches which are contained within the original revelation we have received in Christ, but which are opened out to us only in the process of following that revelation into ever new circumstances. One of the ways in which Williams tries to speak about this process is by comparing it with the process of the poetic exploration and expansion of a language.[32]

Human beings are, Williams suggests, fundamentally linguistic creatures, in a broad sense. We are, that is, creatures who inhabit and act in the world, and to act in the world requires us to see the stuff around us not simply as a bewildering variety of pure sense-impressions, but to see it as objects or circumstances with which we can remember interacting, objects or circumstances that come with future possibilities, objects or circumstances that we can imagine altering. We are inherently and unavoidably involved in discriminating one object or circumstance from another, and in seeing such objects and circumstances as having *meanings*.

Staring in front of me now, I see a patch of grey with a strange, luminous patch of blue within it, and within the patch of blue a white rectangle speckled with black marks. Or rather, that's not what I see, unless I squint: I actually see a computer monitor, with a blue 'desktop' pictured on it, and a white document on that desktop, covered with writing. I see it, in other words, as something I can understand and work with – as containing possibilities for action. I remember working with such things before, and I can imagine ways in which I can manipulate it now. I see it not as a meaningless pattern of colours, but rather as bearing all sorts of meanings. Of course, I had to *learn* to see the thing in front of me as a computer screen, and even more had to learn to see it as implying possibilities of action. And there was a long process during which my perceptions of this object sharpened and developed: when what was originally simply clutter at the edges of what I was seeing resolved itself into further objects with further meanings, presenting further possibilities for action. I learnt to see the small pictures on the desktop as 'icons' that I could click on, and so on. In other words, the meanings which enable me to work with this one small part of my experience have not been static – I have continually learnt to see new ways of acting, new possibilities in the objects and circumstances around me, to make new discriminations – to find new *meanings*. Yet that does not mean that there has been a free-for-all, a random flux of meanings: there has, rather, been something like a deepening and a complexifying of some basic meanings learnt early on – a process of innovation and change, certainly, but in exploration of a framework already provided by some early and central intuitions. I can see myself as having learnt, explored, and extended a *language* which enables me to interact with this part of the world in richer and more complex ways – both literally (I have learnt words like 'desktop', 'icon', 'monitor') and more metaphorically – I have learnt this whole range of new meanings, and some of the 'grammar' of those meanings. It is because I inhabit this patchwork of connected words and ideas that I am able to work with the object in front of me in productive and interesting ways.

Crucially, learning and extending the 'language' by which I

am able to interact with this machine does not close down my options: it *creates* options; it creates new possibilities of action. When faced with a grey lump of plastic to which I can give no meanings, a lump which is not described and caught up in the webs of my language, I am not in a position of sovereign freedom with respect to it: I am impotent. Only when it gets caught up in my language, and becomes meaningful to me, can I work with it – no longer as a grey lump but as a computer. Acquiring language, fixing some meanings, is what gives me the freedom to think and to act; and each new element that I learn allows me – if I do not get scared – to refine and extend my action, and also puts me in a position where I can learn even more; the more I see, the more I am able to experiment and play and discover.

My computer is a pretty limited part of the world, and is one of the more controllable parts of it. It is, after all, a machine – and I may run into problems, but there are such things as help-lines and technical experts, and I can (ever optimistic) reasonably expect that someone will know *the answer* if I run into a problem. But what is true of me and my computer monitor is more generally true: our world is, Williams says, continually being 'brought . . . into meaningfulness';[33] we learn a 'language' (broadly speaking) which enables us to interact with the world in certain ways and which also enables us to experiment and explore, to push at the edges of that language, seeking to discover new meanings and possibilities of action. This process is sometimes more haphazard and argumentative than has been the case (most of the time) with my computer: such is the restless nature of human beings that any proposed meaningful structure calls forth amendment, response, and modification; as soon as somebody has said, 'This is how it works, this is what this means', we are apt to respond by saying, 'Yes, but what if we see it this way. . .?' '[W]e work on our world in what seems an insatiable desire for new perception and new possibilities of action.'[34] But just as with my computer, there are always constraints on the sprouting of meanings – however I think about it, this computer is never going to pop downstairs and make me a cup of tea, and the world in general is just as intractable – though that does not mean that change can never be dramatic: think of the change in meaning which leads from seeing this extendable flap over here not as the computer's drinks holder but as its CD player.

It is in this context that Williams speaks about the role of *poets* – meaning by that, I think, rather more than simply 'those who publish verse'. The job of a poet is to help make the world significant – to find ways of speaking which enable us to see aspects of the world in new ways, or to see aspects of the world which our current ways of speaking and thinking obscure, and so to allow us to imagine different possibilities of action and response, different futures. A poet can only perform this function if he or she has learnt an existing language well, has become immersed in it – in order to be able to press towards its edges, and to find things which that language *almost* allows us to say, by discovering ways of saying them. The poet knows that our normal ways of speaking are both what enable our life in the world, and what limit it – and so the poet travels to the borderlands of our language in the hope of helping us to discover ways beyond those limits, or at least ways to discover aspects of reality which we are not yet able to speak, and which pose to us a task of exploration and discovery.

I have explained all this at some length because I think it helps us to understand one of Williams' characteristic ways of thinking about the Christian tradition. We can think of the revelation in Christ as a revelation which transforms certain key meanings in the language by which we live in the world – not, now, a transformation which enables us to see the drinks holder as a CD player, but a much deeper one which enables us to see ourselves as loved. We can see it as something which gives us, in other words, the rudiments of a new language – and so as something which *enables* our exploration, our questioning, our innovation. ('Only tradition makes thinking possible', he says at one point.)[35] From that point on, we may think of the Christian tradition as the exploration and extension of this language – an exploration in which we find ways to use it to speak about more and more of the world, to make finer and finer discriminations. And if we see it like this, that process of extension will not simply be seen as the *application* of a received truth to a wide range of situations: it will be seen as a journey of discovery in which we simultaneously explore the world and delve more deeply into the meanings which are latent in the language we are originally given in the Gospel.

We learn this language, and learn to live in the world by means of it – but by indwelling it we learn the limitations of our current speaking of it, and are called to find new ways of speaking it. The Christian tradition, Williams suggests, is therefore, in a sense, 'cumulative'; it consists of

> a constantly expanding network of narratives, biographies. The more such narratives are seen as illustrations, subordinate to a governing theoretical structure [i.e. seen as speech which simply illustrates the current state of the language], the more the tradition closes in on itself, offering self-justifying projections rather than the risk of incarnation. The more these stories are seen as fresh statements (new metaphors?) in a common tongue, the more the tradition shows itself to be a living – and therefore an incomplete – thing. To some extent, new classics displace old, new statements make older ones problematic: perhaps we cannot 'talk' like that now. Yet the language remains, carrying with it a history of expressive extension and increasing distinctiveness . . . And the idea of 'orthodoxy' is what evolves as the common life gropes for a sense of the criteria for continuity . . . the 'grammar' by which we can discern that even wildly divergent utterances are being made in one and the same language.[36]

This is a powerful way of seeing the Christian tradition; but it is, as Williams says, bound to make us ask about *continuity*, about faithfulness to the source of the language in Jesus Christ, those foundational meanings which gave us this new language in the first place. Can we make sense of the claim that we are still speaking the same language as earlier generations of Christians, even though our language has been modified and elaborated over time, shifting literally from Aramaic to Greek to Latin to English (say), and shifting in more subtle but no less significant ways as well? Are there ways in which we can *test* proposed innovations and alterations to our language?

V

It is at this point that we must speak about doctrine: about the Church's hard-won statements of recognized teaching – and its equally hard-won rejection of false teachings. (We might think, for example, of the doctrines of the Incarnation and the Trinity; much of the discussion of the previous two chapters could be understood as a reflection upon – an attempt to explain the propriety and necessity of – those two doctrines: 'There is but one living and true God, everlasting, without body parts or passions . . . and in unity of this Godhead there be three Persons, of one substance, power and eternity; the Father, the Son, and the Holy Ghost' and 'The Son, which is the Word of the Father, begotten from everlasting of the Father . . . took Man's nature in the womb of the blessed Virgin . . .' – to quote from the first two Anglican Articles of Religion.) Doctrine has to do with faithfulness; it has to do with ensuring that the unavoidable innovations and alterations in our Christian language do not prevent us from speaking the original question which the Church hears from Jesus. Those innovations and alterations are necessary if we are to speak the Christian language in contexts beyond its starting-point, but the development of doctrine is intended to ensure that it is still *Christian* language that we speak in those new places; it is therefore intended to hold open 'the possibility of preaching Jesus as a questioning and converting presence in ever more diverse cultures and periods'.[37] If that sounds rather abstract, Williams says more concretely that

> The slow and difficult evolution of a doctrinal language, creeds and definitions . . . [has] to do at heart with maintaining the possibility of speaking about a God who becomes unreservedly accessible in the person of Jesus Christ and in the life of

Christ's community. What is rejected is, pretty consistently, any teaching that leaves God only provisionally or partially involved in the communicating of the new life of grace and communion.[38]

More pithily, Williams can say that 'all doctrine [is], essentially, reflection on Easter'[39] and that 'the job of doctrine is to *hold us still* before Jesus'.[40] As the previous two chapters have tried to show, he believes, for instance, that the credal doctrines of Trinity and Incarnation are appropriate implications of, and necessary supports for, the preaching of the Gospel of Jesus of Nazareth.

Doctrinal creeds, statements, and definitions, although apparently delivered to us on a plate, actually emerged from a slow and often painful process of reflection upon the diverse and unsystematic language with which our tradition began, particularly as that language was taken up in the community's worship and devotion, probing and testing until the deepest constraints which hold that language together became visible.[41] Doctrinal reflection investigates the extent to which 'The openness, the "impropriety", the *play* of liturgical imagery [for example] is anchored to a specific set of commitments as to the limits and defining conditions within which the believing life is lived'; and it attempts to find ways to 'characterize these defining conditions'.[42] In the case of the doctrine of the Incarnation, for example:

> Given a commitment to the truthfulness of the whole complex of practices, verbal and non-verbal, moral, imaginative, devotional, and reflective, which embody 'the church's conviction' about Jesus, dogmatic Christological definition sets out to establish the conditions for telling this truth in the most comprehensive, least conceptually extravagant and least idly mythological language.[43]

The development of doctrine, therefore, is a way in which the Church points to a reality which is not in its control, but which provides the context in which it lives – and which therefore imposes some kind of constraints upon what we say and do. We are *answerable* for our speech and action, we are *responsible* to a reality which we do not master. The development of doctrine is a way in which the Church indicates that its language is not its own, for it to alter as it sees fit, but a gift. It is a reminder that Christian language is not a medium of unfettered free expression, but rather a medium in which we are called to hear and speak the truth.

> Doctrine is about our end (and our beginning); about what in our humanity is not negotiable, dispensable, vulnerable to revision according to political convenience or cultural choice and fashion . . . Doctrine purports to tell us what we are for, and what the shape is of a life lived in accordance with the way things are, and how such a life becomes accessible to us, even in the middle of the corruption and unfreedom of a shadowed history.[44]

In performing this function, however, doctrine brings its own dangers. It speaks to us of that movement towards God in which we are caught up, but it can too easily betray the character of that movement by domesticating it:

> the history of doctrine has the paradoxical character of a repeated effort of definition designed to counter the ill effects of definition itself – rather like the way in which a good poet will struggle to find a fixed form of words that will decisively avoid narrowing and lifeless fixtures or closures of meaning.[45]

And the 'ill effects of definition itself' do sometimes gain the upper hand. Doctrine can be made to speak in a voice which denies our 'openness to judgement', our vulnerability before the searching questioning of Christ. When we forget its role in 'holding open the question', 'holding us still before Jesus', reminding us of the freeing constraints which make our life possible – when 'we begin instead to use this language to defend ourselves, to denigrate others, to control and correct – . . . then it becomes a problem'.[46] If we are to avoid this problem, then the Church's dogmatic activity, its attempts to structure its public and common language in such a way that the possibilities of judgement and renewal are not buried, must constantly be chastened by the awareness that it so acts in order to give place to the freedom of God – the freedom of God from the Church's sense of itself and its power, and thus the freedom of God to renew and absolve. This is why dogmatic language becomes empty and even destructive of faith when it is isolated from a lively and converting worship and a spirituality that is not afraid of silence and powerlessness.[47]

Nevertheless, Williams does think that it is appropriate to be serious about doctrine, and even to talk about 'heresy'. Heresy is any attempt to clean up or rearrange Christian language which results in a 'major reduction in the range of available resources of meaning'.[48] It normally arises when those engaged in the development of doctrine privilege conceptual economy and precision over richness of symbolic resource – when they make the attempt to tie things down too neatly, to *control* the various and excessive language of worship and devotion too closely. Or heresy can arise when the attempt is made, wittingly or unwittingly, to shrink a tradition of devotion and worship 'to the dimension of one person's or one group's need, for comfort or control'.[49] Heresy is any drastic reduction in the *capaciousness* of Christian language – the resource which it provides for making sense, and for asking questions, in any and every situation. It is any too strong culling of orthodoxy's rich and diverse 'doctrinal ecology', 'a variety of theological discourse wide enough to communicate the full and disorienting significance of the generative theological experience'.[50] Returning to the analogy with language and poetry: heresy for Williams is not like the speaker who peppers his speech with hanging prepositions and split infinitives, prompting angry letters from grammatical sticklers; it is more like the cancerous spreading of 'the deadness of bureaucratic jargon, the deadness of uplifting waffle, the deadness of acronyms and target setting' – language which 'flattens out the depth' of human life, which deprives us of 'a resource for the extremities

of experience, obsessive passion or jealousy, adoration, despair',
'missing "keys" in our music'.[51]

Williams believes, for instance, that the 'Arian' theology which
was condemned at Nicaea, by the framers of the first draft of
our Nicene Creed – a theology which would have rejected what
we said about incarnation at the start of this section, and which
was eventually declared heretical in the debates of the early
Church – would have been decisively less able to cope with the
changes in intellectual climate which the West has undergone
in the centuries since. He believes that, although it was in many
ways a theology more precise, more clear, more *explicable* in the
culture of its time, it achieved that precision only by binding itself
too tightly to one particular intellectual milieu, and by trimming
the traditional language of worship and devotion too drastically
in order not to offend that milieu. To 'hold open the question'
which Christians are charged to carry will involve us not simply
in proposing doctrinal ways of pointing to the non-negotiable
context of our life and language, but also in testing any such
proposal seriously and carefully, and, potentially, rejecting some
proposals as 'heretical'.

VI

I spoke earlier in this chapter of the Church as 'the community
of those being formed around Christ, of those being made into
reflections of Christ to one another . . . a vast collection of refractions of the light of Christ into the rainbow of billions of diverse
faces, each of which helps us by the particular partial light that it
reflects to see more of the glory of God in the face of Christ'. We
are now in a position to explore more thoroughly what Williams
says on these themes.

Jesus, we have been saying, calls us to share his life, and the life
which he shares with us is a life of self-giving. If we are drawn into
this life of self-giving, then it will be by *ourselves* becoming self-
givers – and that means that our selves will become *gifts* – gifts to
God, and gifts to each other. To put it another way, we could say

that to be drawn into the life of Christ is to become those who pass on that life, by embodying that life in our own distinctive ways: the medium of the giving is our own lives; what we give is a reflection of the life of Christ in our particular circumstances – the life that emerges when his whole life is brought to bear on each of our whole lives. We become those whose lives give God's life – and that is what it means to be Church. 'To belong in the apostolic community is to be involved in a complex act of giving away: to be at the disposal of God's will, to give away the life we have, so that God's life can be given through us.'[52]

If the Church is a place in which we learn the Gospel, a place where we learn the nature of God's gift, then it is so primarily because, as those who live grounded in Scripture, propelled by the sacraments, and held open by doctrine, we teach the Gospel to each other, and learn it from each other. We learn to see the face of Christ in the faces of those who share his life, and who share his life with us. And that means also that being called into the life of Christ means being called to become recipients – recipients of the gifts which all the other members of Christ's Church become to us; recipients of what they show us of Christ. We are called to 'the opening of the individual subject to the wealth of communal life and thought'.[53] (And this, by the way, is why it is not simply a throw-away nicety when Williams says, in the Introduction to his doctoral thesis, that 'Anything of value in the pages that follow belongs not to me but to the catholic communion of minds in Christ, mediated to me by my teachers and friends' – he was aware that he received the Gospel from others, and that whatever exploration and explanation of it he might undertake himself was fundamentally the unwrapping of a gift that he had received from those others.)

If the Gospel is learnt in this way – by the exchange of these gifts within the community – then we must be very wary of any way of talking or acting which seems to imply that one group of Christians already *possesses* Christ, and so does not need to receive him from others. To say that would be to cease to be recipients, and so to close ourselves off from some of the riches of Christ. It would be to cease *learning*.

This in turn means that we must be very wary of judging other members of the community. God 'leads Moses in Moses's way and Arsenius in Arsenius's way' and 'no man has the right to judge another's standing before God', Williams says.[54]

But this is not to abandon a concern with 'orthodoxy', as if anything goes, and as if we must be prepared to accept anything that anybody says about Christ, or any way that discipleship to Christ is lived out by others. What we are hoping to receive from others is more of Christ, and there is only one Christ – and so we are called continually to search for *how* other Christian lives relay Christ's life to us; to hunt for the unity between all these diverse representations.[55] Nevertheless, if we reject the idea that any one group already possesses the whole of Christ, and may simply measure other groups against the yardstick of its own existing possession, then the unity which we seek will not be obvious, or instantly grasped. 'Only in the activity of conversation do we find what the depths and what the limits are of our common language, what it is that holds us together as sharers in one world.'[56] My understanding of Christ may be challenged by yours, and yours by mine – but it is only by discussing, by arguing, by returning to the Scriptures together, that we can hope to discover what is central and what peripheral, what must be rejected and what affirmed. Even those who we – perhaps rightly – condemn as heretics may have something to teach us of the nature of the Gospel which they too are trying to understand. Williams once again takes the debates of the fourth century as his example:

> The long-term credibility and sustainability of the Nicene faith may have something to do with the degree to which it succeeds – usually more or less unwittingly – in subsuming and even deepening the Christian concerns of the teachers it sets out to condemn . . . the implication being that, in any doctrinal conflict, theologians are not likely to know with total clarity what the doctrinal (and concrete ecclesial) forms will be that will succeed in most comprehensively holding the range of proper and defensible Christian interests involved in the

conflict. There is no absolute *locus standi* above the struggle
. . . Orthodoxy continues to be *made*.[57]

A passion for orthodoxy, then, for right teaching and right
learning of the Gospel, will take the form not of soap-box
shouting, but of *ecumenism* – of building serious conversations
between Christians who differ, not settling for platitudes which
cover up the differences between us, but challenging one another
and learning from one another in the hope of discovering more
of the riches of Christ in one another. Williams argues that the
very idea of 'orthodoxy' emerged in the early Christian centuries
precisely from the attempt made by various Christian churches
to recognize in one another the same Christ that they themselves
worshipped. That is, the very idea of 'orthodoxy' emerged in the
second and third centuries as a distinction arose between strands
of Christianity for which communication between congregations
was an ad hoc and occasional affair, and strands in which there
were 'regular and significant links' to the point of 'an almost
obsessional mutual interest and interchange' between congregations – links sustained by mutual visiting, by the calling of
common meetings, and by the exchange of letters.[58] Much of the
exchange took the form of argument and criticism – this was no
smooth harmony. But the arguments took place because these
congregations believed that they were exploring a common heritage, that they were hearers of a common Gospel – it *mattered* that
they could not yet see the unity between their differing positions.
The debates were long, arduous, and frequently deeply riven by
conflict. But it is out of that crucible that orthodoxy takes shape,
as the participants struggle to discover doctrinal forms 'that will
succeed in most comprehensively holding the range of proper
and defensible Christian interest involved in the conflict'.[59]

If we now seek to learn a capacious orthodoxy faithful to the
Gospel, it cannot be by defending some sacred deposit of truth
granted only to us against all comers. We are not champions of
orthodoxy if we simply declare ourselves ready to shout down
anyone who differs: that would be to defend a sectionalism
which is a profound denial of the Gospel – a refusal to participate

in the life which Christ shares with us. Rather, we seek to learn a generous orthodoxy by engaging in serious conversation, serious argument over Scripture, in the light of the sacraments, with those who differ from us. We engage in conversation both with those who differ from us now and with those Christians of past ages whose awkward and uncomfortable Christianity we meet in our history books and sometimes in our hymns and liturgies. Those others in space and time, with whom we do not easily agree, are the face of Christ to us, and to ignore them or shout them down (or to patronize them or effectively ignore them with spineless acceptance) is to disfigure that face.

Chapter Four

Adulthood and Childhood

I

At about the same time that Rowan Williams' name was popping up everywhere in connection with the Canterbury job, another story was appearing both in newspapers' religion slots and in their ordinary news pages. Everyone was talking about Philip Pullman's *Dark Materials* trilogy – and about the books' apparent attack on organized religion. In interview after interview, Pullman explained that he had wished to avoid the terrible mistake made by an earlier writer of children's fantasy, C. S. Lewis, who, Pullman said, had not allowed his characters to grow up – who in *The Last Battle* had barred his character Susan from the kingdom of heaven because she became interested in lipstick and nylons and put childish adventures behind her ('She always was a jolly sight too keen on being grown up'), and who had brutally contrived that his main characters should be able to remain in that kingdom permanently as children ('"There *was* a real railway accident," said Aslan softly, " . . . and all of you are – as you used to call it in the Shadowlands – dead. The term is over, the holidays have begun."').[1] *His Dark Materials*, in contrast, ends with a vision Pullman calls the republic of heaven, which the central child characters enter precisely by maturing, entering adolescence, waking up to the fact that they are sexual beings – and by taking full responsibility for living in the real world, Lewis' Shadowlands, rather than in a deferred heaven.

> The kingdom was over, the kingdom of heaven, it was all finished. We shouldn't live as if it mattered more than this life

in this world, because where we are is always the most important place . . . We have to be all those difficult things like cheer-
ful and kind and curious and brave and patient, and we've got
to study and think, and work hard, all of us, in all our different
worlds, and then we'll build . . . the republic of heaven.[2]

Williams recognizes the force of a challenge like Pullman's – not
necessarily against Lewis, but against Christianity. It all too often
does seem to be true that 'The gospel degrades human beings,
feeding them with sweets like children; it will not let them grow
up' – will not allow them to take adult responsibility for their
action in the world.[3] But this is precisely the kind of easy Gospel
that Williams denies, so it is no surprise to find running through
his work a very different vision of adulthood – a vision of a proper
maturity, nurtured by the Gospel rather than endlessly deferred
by it – and a concern with the protection of the kind of childhood
that can prepare us for this adulthood. 'Every proper proclamation of the Easter gospel', Williams says, represents a rejection of
'infantilism', and a 'call to "adulthood"'.[4] The Gospel calls us to
an adulthood defined by gratitude and by openness to judgement
– by God's acceptance, and by God's disarming of our selfishness.
It is not, therefore, an adulthood that consists in rock-solid independence, in wanting and needing nothing, in possessing an
identity that is complete and secure; it is not an adulthood that
has left behind receiving or learning. Rather, adulthood, for
Williams, consists in 'being daily grasped in . . . helplessness'.[5]

The call to adulthood is not a call to isolation, but a call to
become unreservedly a giver and a receiver – to be caught up
totally into the economy of giving which I described in the last
chapter. '[T]he resurrection gospel', Williams says, 'speaks of the
proper expectation – the right – of all men and women to responsible identity, the capacity to be self-aware agents empowered to
take active part in the "net of exchange"'[6] – the 'net' of giving
and receiving.[7] In different words, borrowed from the Russian
Orthodox theologians whom he studied early in his career, it
is a divine call, an invitation to become fully 'personal', where
'personal' means something like 'constituted by what we receive

from others and by what we give in return'. In still other words, it is a call to the life of the spirit.

> '[F]lesh', as St. Paul uses that term, is . . . a word that describes human life minus relationship. Or perhaps . . . human life that is not properly inhabited. Flesh is human life somehow alien-ated, cut off from its environment, cut off from the life of spirit which in St. Paul's usage is always about relation . . . The gift of the spirit in St. Paul's theology is a gift that always brings relation. And the life of the spirit, as opposed to the life of the flesh, is life in free relation to God and generous relation to one another.[8]

The story of our growing up, our becoming adult, is, therefore,

> Not simply . . . a record of what happened to this particular lump of fat and bone. You can tell your story as a story of how you learned to speak and to relate, to respond and to interact . . . the story of how your life, how your flesh, became inhab-ited.[9]

Williams can also speak of this as our flesh becoming filled with *meaning*. Instead of being 'a lump of untenanted material which lies around for other people to fall over' our body can become 'a language . . . a means of communication' – it can be caught up in the 'conversation' of giving and receiving, of relationship and interaction. It will turn out, as we pursue these themes, that this is the core of Williams' understanding of adulthood: the call to become *meaningful flesh*.

My writing of this book has been wonderfully interrupted and delayed by the arrival of a daughter, who as I write these words is only a few weeks old. She is, at this age, quite properly 'infan-tile', and there are two aspects of that which become especially clear when she cries. She mostly cries when she is hungry, and is demanding milk as the one thing in all the world which can make her happy; and – however little she might be capable of doing on her own – she *demands* at the top of her lungs that the world give her what she wants. That is, large parts of her waking life are structured by desire for something very specific, which gratifies her desire when it appears – and in trying to compel the universe to deliver what she desires, without any regard to whether other bits of the universe might have plans of their own (like finishing books by the publishers' deadline, for instance). And all this is entirely appropriate behaviour for a baby: the problem comes when grown-ups behave in the same way.

We are beset, in the first place, by the infantile temptation to imagine ourselves on the verge of completeness. If I just had *that* thing, we say, I would be happy; I wouldn't need anything more. I look at myself, calculate the size and shape of the gaps in my life, and then hunt for the things or people or experiences that will fill them. But, Williams says, 'grace is incalculable'.[10] Grace – the gift of God's life which we receive through Christ, and through those around us – does not gratify; it will overflow any neat hole that we expect it to fill, and will burst apart the seams of areas of our life we thought stable and finished. And grace can't be sucked from a nipple, providing just the amounts of comfort we think we need. To be caught up in grace is to be caught up in a whirl of giving and receiving which is, by the standards of gratification, always excessive. The gifts which the Gospel offers to us can't be 'planned and packaged by my ego' – they can't be the kind of gifts we go and buy for ourselves before informing the supposed giver how much they have spent on us. They are not a neat completion, but an invasion of the familiar landscape of our selves by saving difference. I constantly try 'in idleness, selfishness or fear, to absorb that saving difference into the familiar contours of my own inner geography' – to establish myself in firm control of what is given to us, in firm control of where it goes and what it does – but grace defeats me.[11]

Adulthood, then, is a matter of the right functioning of desire. Our infantile temptation is to see ourselves as having only specific, completable lacks – specific, controllable desires. We desire to fill those lacks, and so we desire the end of desire – we desire a move from desire to satisfaction. Grace faces us with a different vision of what it is to be a functioning self. 'The self becomes adult and truthful in being faced with the *incurable* character of its desire: the world is such that *no* thing will bestow on the self a rounded and finished identity.'[12] Grace awakens us to a vision of the self not as controllable and nearly complete, but as continually being given more, continually receiving not just neatly packaged extras, but transformation, real growth, unexpected reordering, from others who genuinely *are* others, rather than projections of our own desires. Grace invites us, as we have said, into an economy of giving which is grounded ultimately in the complete self-giving of God. To be adult in such a world is to be drawn by God into an unending drama of desire: a continual longing for more of God, more that we cannot control; a continual longing not for the completion and closing of our selves but for the 'steady and endless enlarging of the heart';[13] a continual desire for the gifts given to us by others who are not our playthings, who never provide us only with what we already knew we wanted – and, reciprocally, a continual discovery that we too can become givers to others.

We are also beset by the infantile temptation to suppose that what we most need is *control* – that we will be adult when we have learnt to impose our will upon our surroundings (or at least on some personal sphere carved out of our surroundings). This is the temptation to imagine that adulthood consists in establishing and extending the arena in which we have sovereign freedom of choice. Williams paints an uncomfortable picture of what might happen in a world which thought in terms of such self-sufficiency, a world where 'what finally secured my identity was . . . the exercise of my will'. It would be a world in which there would be 'all kinds of difficulty about appealing as a moral sanction to the danger of diminishing the solidity of the self by ignoring the perceptions of others' – for how could such an appeal be anything other than the imposition of others' wills over my own? It would be a world in which sorrow or remorse over destructive action was replaced with 'the dread of embarrassment . . . the fear of losing public plausibility' – i.e., a world in which someone found to be doing wrong would probably concentrate largely upon the 'possible disadvantages, weakenings of a negotiating position in the sphere of public transactions' which his or her action might produce – the damage which it might do to the effectiveness of his or her *will*. And it would be a world in which 'You would expect an immense investment of energy in strengthening the image of the willing or choosing subject, whether by a therapeutic rhetoric of "feeling strong" in the face of adverse circumstances, or by a market environment encouraging ideas of free-floating consumer liberty.' 'You would, in short, expect an environment rather like the contemporary North Atlantic world.'[14] This infantile temptation is alive and flourishing in our culture.

Williams argues that a vision of adulthood dominated by freedom and control is a denial of the lack of independence that characterizes all our action.

> [H]uman activity is misunderstood if it is seen as a sequence of 'responsible' decisions taken by a conscious and self-aware person, in control of his life. More often it is a confused, partly conscious, partly (as we say) instinctive response to the givenness of a world we do not dominate, a world of histories and ideas, languages and societies, structures we have not built. More perhaps than we ever realise or accept with our minds, we are being acted upon as much as acting.[15]

Our ability to act is a result of our having learnt a language through which we can respond to the world, a language which shapes our responsiveness, giving it more or less discrimination, more or less resilience. Our ability to act therefore *depends* upon what we have received, *depends* upon others having acted upon us. We act by means of the gifts we have been given.

And so 'my past, my publicly identifiable history, the story that can be told of me, does not *belong* exclusively to me'. And this is not just true in the sense that I receive the ability to act from others: 'My actions have had effects and meanings I never foresaw or intended; even the meanings I *did* intend have become involved with the speech and the story of other lives.'[16] To see control as the essence of 'adulthood' is to imagine that we are only truly ourselves to the extent that we have *made* ourselves: to the extent that we have managed to create some space which is ours alone, and has not been interfered with or shaped by other people; it supposes that we are only truly ourselves to the extent that we have managed to preserve some part of our life which is not 'given' by anyone but ourselves. Ultimately, this vision of control, the vision of the triumph of the will, is another way of denying the pervasiveness of giving and receiving; to think of there being any sphere in which we are free from being acted upon, free to be the only and absolute giver of meaning, free from the unintended consequences of our actions, is a destructive illusion. I need to be taught, in the face of this temptation, that even my 'self' is something given to me, something I receive from others.

> The gospel of the resurrection proposes that 'possession' is precisely the wrong, the corrupt and corrupting, metaphor for our finding place in the world. What we 'possess', must go; we must learn to be what we receive from God in the vulnerability of living *in* (not above) the world of change and chance.[17]

Williams' vision of adulthood, then, is a 'vision of a universe in which reasoned control or liberated desire is not ultimate'.[18] His vision is of an adulthood characterized by

> a commitment of trust in God's compassion that shows itself in costly and painful *letting go* of the obsessions of the self – both the obsessive search for the perfectly satisfying performance and the obsessive search for the perfectly unconstrained experience.[19]

The Gospel calls us to recognize 'the breakdown of performance and the emptiness of gratification'.[20]

In other words, the Gospel does not call us to an *escape* from the world – an escape from materiality and dependence. As bodily and social creatures in a material world our wills are *necessarily* constrained – they can't simply get what they want, but must work with the world, paying attention to its constraints; our wills are 'bound to conscious adaptation, self-modification, reflective and deliberate activity'.[21] And as bodily and social creatures in a material world, we are bound to find that the world doesn't simply deliver itself to us in packages the size of our perceived desires. (And this, by the way, is why Williams considers himself committed to some kind of philosophical 'realism' – i.e., precisely to a view which sees the world around us as intractable stuff that resists our attempts to categorize and predict it: we recognize ourselves as 'addressed' by the stuff of the world rather than having it entirely at our disposal, and therefore as required to work with the world rather than simply on it, and as facing the possibility that our projects in the world will fail.[22]) Rather than thinking that the constraints of finitude and bodiliness are constraints to be overcome – by, perhaps, refinements of our control, or by increased access to the objects which gratify us – the Gospel calls us to accept our finitude; it 'assists us in *being mortal*, living in the constraints of a finite and material world without resentment'.[23] It calls us, that is, to become more truthful, more open-eyed inhabitants of the world. The Christian vision is not of the soul being stripped of its body, and so stripped of the limitations and frustrations and rebuffs of mortality, but rather of the body becoming, as I said earlier, more fully inhabited, more fully relational. And Williams argues that, however much it has from time to time been a note sounded uncertainly by Christians, Christian theology has from its earliest years required us to value bodiliness and finitude. Christians have, however falteringly, found that the Scriptures they have inherited, the stories of incarnation and bodily resurrection that they believe, and the rites of baptism and of Eucharist that they practise, make more sense if we assume that the Gospel has to do with the drawing of creaturely beings – souls *and* bodies, inhabited flesh – into relationship with a transcendent God.[24]

The Christian vision holds out a hope not of escape but of redemption. It does not, that is, give us the hope of an escape or rescue *from* bodiliness, finitude, and creatureliness, but the hope of the salvation *of* bodiliness, finitude, and creatureliness. It holds out a vision in which 'Our language and our bodies will not be mechanisms for isolating ourselves, but will be the sharing of God with each other, the showing to one another of the divine freedom and creative mercy . . . We shall be to each other not idols but icons, effective signs of God's transfiguration of the world.'[25] It holds out a vision not of the stripping away of flesh, but of flesh become meaningful.

II

One aspect of Williams' understanding of adulthood is the mature acceptance, nurtured by the Gospel, that our finitude and weakness and dependence are not things we need to escape; it is an acceptance, that is, of our *incompleteness*. Seen from another direction, however, this turns out to be a concern for *wholeness*: a hope that our whole selves can become 'icons, effective signs of God's transfiguration of the world'. The Gospel assures me that my whole self – the self which I have become, which I have been given, which includes all the grit and moss that I have picked up – is the 'concern and the theatre of God's saving work',[26] and that it can, by God's grace, 'become the way in which God speaks in Christ-like form to the world now'.[27]

Sometimes, when we come to God in prayer, we might picture ourselves as a little like a schoolboy called before a teacher, and forced to empty his pockets of all the bits and pieces he has accumulated – the catapult, the conker, the comic, the cigarette cards – before he is allowed again to sit in class. We assume that the self that is allowed to pray is the self that has discarded all its distractions, involvements, complications, worries, and histories – all the baggage that it has picked up, all the history that gets in the way. But Williams suggests that 'when God pulls taut the slack thread of desire, binding it to himself, the muddled and painful litter of experience is gathered together and given direction';[28] it is not discarded. On the journey to God,

people come by roundabout routes, with complex histories,

sin and muddle and false perceptions and wrong starts. It's no good saying to them, 'You must become simple and whole-hearted', as if this could be done just by wishing it. The real question is, 'Can you take all your complicated history with you on a journey towards the manger?'

'[D]on't deny the tangle and the talents, the varied web of what has made you who you are. Every step is part of the journey; on this journey, even the false starts are part of the journey.' We should not try to forget all this dubious material before coming to pray, nor should we pray for God to burn it all away, but rather should say, 'Use what my experience and my mistakes and false starts have made me in order to let your transfiguring love show through.'[29]

Of course, it remains true that there is no way towards God which does not involve us dealing with 'our great load of arrogant self-reliance, bluster, noisy fear and fantasy'[30] – but the process in which that shedding takes place is not one in which we cease to be ourselves, or one in which we are severed from our history. It is one in which those selves, with their histories, are redeemed. The forgiveness, the acceptance, which meets us in the Gospel is one which sees all this mess that we are in – all this mess that we *are* – and sees what it can become, how it can be transformed, how it can be made to shine. What we are given by God's acceptance is '*hope*, the apprehension of present truth, present reality as infinitely open to the transfiguring and glorifying action of God'.[31]

Williams' central biblical example for all this is Simon Peter's encounter with the risen Jesus in Galilee. Having betrayed Jesus three times, he is deliberately reminded by Jesus of his betrayal.

> Simon has to recognize himself as betrayer: that is part of the past that makes him who he is. If he is to be called again, if he can again become a true apostle, the 'Peter' that he is in the purpose of Jesus rather than the Simon who runs back into the cosy obscurity of 'ordinary' life, his failure must be assimilated, lived through again and brought to good and not to destructive issue.[32]

Jesus invites Peter to discover that his betrayal has not broken the call which God has for him. He is invited to discover that Jesus 'accepts, forgives, bears and absolves the hurt done',[33] and that he can take Peter the betrayer and make him the feeder of his sheep. What Peter receives is not 'innocence' – the pretence that his betrayal did not happen – but transfiguring *grace*.[34]

Grace, then – God's gift in the Gospel – is not the gift of forgetfulness; it does not enable us to pretend that our past has never happened. Like Jesus on the lake shore, it *reminds* us of our history, takes us through it again, but invites us to see what the person who did all this, who is broken in all these ways, can become. I am called by the Gospel to 'the slow and difficult processes of learning new ways of seeing and speaking my history' – learning new ways in which the self which *is* this history can become an icon of God in the world.[35] And this learning is a process in which my self continues to be *made*. It is not the unlocking of an innocent self locked away behind this history, essentially unaffected by it; it is the transformation of the self which is this history; it is this self re-worked, moulded in new ways. Williams is deeply concerned to avoid a model of self-understanding which he thinks would make nonsense of all of this. That is the way of thinking which tells us that, beneath all the grime and mess and complication on the surface, deep inside we have an innocent or authentic self which we can discover with the right therapy, with the right kind of mental excavation: a 'core of uncompromised interiority' which 'may be discovered by bracketing out large tracts of the social, the corporate, the linguistic'.[36] Captivated by this model, we are all too capable

> of betraying the reality of what we in fact are, where we in fact stand, of body and speech, of the bonds of sociality that constitute us as human, discounting the tangible, utterable contingency of what is there for the senses, in claiming to strip . . . to what is held to be true and essential.[37]

Our self is not like a Brazil nut, from which we can crack away the hard outer casing in order to find the pure white core inside. The self is more like an onion: if you peel off one skin, you'll find another underneath: an onion is skin all the way down, and the human self is 'body and speech . . . bonds of sociality . . . tangible, utterable contingency' all the way down. We are not sent in quest of the hidden, internal *core* of our selves, but rather directed towards what the whole of our selves can be made into by God, what of God's life they can play out. We can cut ourselves off from this possibility, or we can embrace it – but these are not the same as the denial or discovery of our 'inner' selves. It is better – in this context, at least – to think of yourself as an onion and God as the Master Chef, than to think of God as the nutcracker and yourself as the nut.

Nevertheless Williams can continue to use the language of 'true self'. The making of the self is also a discovery of the self, a process in which our self is *found*: it is a process in which we uncover the self which we are in the purposes of God, the self which God who sees us truly knows us to be, the self which is hid with Christ in God. We are called to the process of 'becoming who we are' – or, we might say, to the process of learning how to see and speak our histories as God sees them, learning how to see and speak our histories truly. I – still caught in self-centred, defensive ways of seeing – see some event from my past as a failure which permanently cripples me, permanently weighs me down; how might it be that God sees it as part of what makes me the person he is saving, part of what makes me the person he is restoring and healing and renewing as an icon of his life in the world? The Gospel calls us to this strange re-imagining of ourselves, this re-telling of our lives, 'striving to construct the narrative least unfaithful to the divine perspective' – and tells us that this is the route by which we discover the truth about ourselves.[38]

It is not, of course, that the Gospel gives us access to a final, complete perspective on ourselves, but rather that in calling us deeper and deeper into himself God is at the same time calling us deeper and deeper into an undistorted self-knowledge. God is, as it were, a conversation partner with whom we can discuss our selves, who constantly prompts us to think again, when we have settled into forgetfulness, or into smug or despairing attitudes towards our past actions and present options.[39] God constantly needles us towards knowledge of our deepest truth; and the 'making' of our self which we undertake with him is not an imposition upon our selves, but their awakening to their true freedom. Think back to the description of Jacob and Esau in the first chapter: Jacob, we said, was understandably worried that Esau consciously or unconsciously was seeking to bend him to his own plan – that Esau was acting strategically rather than entirely openly. So, although it is certainly true that we receive our identity from others (we learn how to think, how to speak, how to act, in interaction with others), there always remains the suspicion that we have not been freed and enabled by what we receive from them, but have rather been *colonized* by it, taken over by their plans and interests. There always remains the suspicion that we are more or less like those slaves who are happy to be slaves, so deeply have they been shaped by a vision of the world and of themselves which serves the interests of the masters. Perhaps we are, in all sorts of ways which of course we cannot see (because they are the very furniture of our minds), enslaved by interests other than our own. Yet we cannot hope to break free into pure self-determination: any attempt to do so would use tools which we had learnt from others, be formulated in language which we inherited from others, and would be open to the very same suspicion that we were once again simply being colonized by others. If we are to be free – if we are not to disappear under the waves of other people's interests – we need to receive ourselves from one who wishes only our good, and is not deceived about that good. So to find our true selves, and to be properly free, requires us to receive our selves from God, to have God as the ultimate conversation-partner on our journey towards coherence.[40] As I said in the second chapter, only God can tell us who we are. Certainly, our journey towards our true selves is one which we can only take with help. We come to know ourselves by means of Bible, by means of tradition, by means of each other – by paying attention to the light of Christ refracted to us by others caught up in the same movement. But it is only as our processes of learning from each other, from the Church, from the tradition, and from the Bible are brought constantly to the foot of the cross that we can be said to be learning the truth about ourselves.

What God will make of me in this process is particular to my history, my bundle of possibilities and problems. Only in the long, slow process in which the whole of my particular life is set on fire by God's particular life can I discover the specific light which God wants my life to shine;[41] only in this way can we discover 'what is our particular way of playing back to God his self-sharing, self-losing care and compassion, the love because of which he speaks and calls in the first place'.[42]

III

Williams suggests that becoming adult, in a Christian sense, will involve us in the careful, prayerful, disciplined nurturing of certain ways of seeing and acting – and that those careful, prayerful disciplines might cluster around at least two foci, which he calls the 'dark night' and 'contemplative pragmatism'. He is not offering a *technique* for becoming adult – a five-point plan which, if you follow it assiduously, will lead you to spiritual success; far from it. After all, to 'operate with a notion of ultimate *success* – even (or especially) when this is ascribed to God' is 'likely to result in crippling self-consciousness'. Rather, we need to acknowledge the 'untidiness and absurdity of pretty well everything we try to do in our discipleship . . .'; the best we can hope for is 'clusters of sound advice and example from those who have no illusions that they are making a proper, let alone a normative, job of it'.[43]

First, then, the 'dark night'. Williams' emphasis falls time and time again on one aspect of the process of learning by which we mature into adulthood – an aspect which he learned above all from John of the Cross and from Luther. We must, if we are to become adults, be weaned from gratification, and that includes being weaned from our attempts to package God and grace as commodities which fit neatly into our world. In particular, we need to be weaned from the notion that God is worth pursuing because of how he makes us feel, or because of how he helps us cope, or because of what he enables us to do. We need to be weaned from any notions that God is worth pursuing *because* of anything else. God is not the means to any end; God *is* the end. To be loved truly, God must be loved for his own sake – or, to put it a different way, God must be loved for nothing.

This is a hard lesson, and it is a lesson we never finish learning; our love always remains impure. One of the central ways in which we begin to learn this lesson, however, is through what has been called 'the dark night of the soul'. The dark night is, or should be, an aspect of all Christian spirituality: the learning of the difficult truth that if God is God, then God is not there for our consolation; a truth learnt primarily by means of the failure of consolation, 'a ruthless purging of self-indulgent and consolatory emotion'.[44] The dark night is not the whole of Christian spirituality, nor should it be – but it should be *present* in all Christian spirituality, because it is a kind of touchstone, a test which asks whether other practices and activities and feelings and thoughts have to do, seriously, with God as God.

> [R]eal dependence on God's grace, real apprehension of God's free action to make us righteous in his eyes, is more evident in the unconsoled endurance of inner turmoil and darkness than in bland confidence that all has been achieved, since the sense of inner darkness turns our attention away from what our minds can register, contain, and be confident of, towards the utterly mysterious love of God.[45]

The 'test of integrity', Williams says, is whether we allow ourselves to be taken into 'the central darkness of the paschal event' – the darkness of the cross.[46]

There are times, and there should be times, when all we can do is cling on to God with 'obstinate blind faithfulness', even though we feel no consolation, even though our prayers seem to disappear into nowhere, even though our words seem empty – even though we can no longer sense the glory of God addressing us in the goodness, truth and beauty of the world.

If God is faithfully present in the glory and the beauty of

creation . . . what's going on when I don't sense that? Well, the
answer is, the same thing is going on. God is going on.[47]

Second: 'contemplative pragmatism', a term coined by Williams. At its heart, this is 'an attitude of time-taking, patient,
absorbing awareness of the particular situation you're in . . . a
willingness to look at apparently secular, apparently unpromising situations, to look long enough and hard enough for God to
come to light . . .'[48]

> [W]e are led by faith both to live in the world, fully flesh and
> blood in it, and at the same time to be aware of the utter
> strangeness of God that waits in the heart of what is familiar
> – as if the world were always on the edge of some total revolu-
> tion, pregnant with a different kind of life, and we were always
> trying to catch the blinding momentary light of its changing
> . . . We, watching and waiting for Christ to come more fully
> to birth in us, are waiting for our lives to become 'iconic', to
> show in their colour and line and movement how God acts,
> Christlike, in us.[49]

God works in and through the messy stuff of the world – other
people, ourselves, the Church, the situations in which we find
ourselves – but what God reveals of Godself through these things
is not something we can safely predict in advance; it is an 'utter
strangeness', a 'revolution', which we will need 'enormous selfless patience' to discern.[50] We will need a willingness to be cor-
rected and judged, and to find that our seeing has hitherto been
distorted by our own selfishness and the selfishness of others.
Contemplative pragmatism explores the world as creation, seeking to see how, despite all the distortions and failures, 'The world
. . . can be sensed as given, the material given us out of which
to make a whole and multi-faceted offering, a gift in return.'[51]
Contemplative pragmatism is the attitude that seeks in every
situation 'To know this moment, this place, this body, this set
of memories, this situation, for what it truly is and to accept this
as reality, the reality with which God at each new instant begins

to work';[52] it is 'the contemplative enterprise of being where we are and refusing the lure of a fantasized future more compliant to our wills'.[53]

Why 'contemplative'? Because anything which is beyond our ability to predict and contain, anything that we can't simply pass over by means of our ordinary habits and stock responses, requires us to *pay attention*. When something different comes along, we have to *learn* how to negotiate it – we have to spend time looking.

> [A]nything which invites us to the pervasive awareness of a world beyond the power of the ego invites contemplation; which is also why contemplation is inseparable from delight and love, which arise in their full reality, life and growth only when we are taken out of the sterile closed circle of ourselves and our plans, projects and expectations.[54]

Williams can even use the much criticized language of 'unworldliness' to describe the attitude he is recommending:

> Christian 'unworldliness' is in fact a way of saying 'yes' to the world by refusing the world's own skewed and destructive account of itself. Christian faith refuses to accept that the only alternatives are those the systems around them can recognize . . . We maintain a stubborn trust that humanity could do its business in other ways and, by telling ourselves the gospel stories and remembering stories of the gospel taking effect in other people's lives, we keep that trust vivid and concrete . . . The Christian task, in the middle of all these struggles and failures, is to try and see situations without the colouring of . . . worldly habits, to see them fresh, to see the flesh and blood of the moment, not the ideologies that draw our gaze away.[55]

Why 'pragmatism'? Because rather than hunting for an impossible gratification, or straining to perfect our will's control – both of which are, as we have said, forms of denial of the finite and creaturely world – contemplative pragmatism acknowledges and works with the constraints and limitations which face us. Contemplative pragmatism involves '*Consenting* to the order of finitude, to limitation and contingency, the endless recalcitrant singularities of things . . . [T]he proper destiny of the will is to embrace its own inevitable frustration by the order of things, and to find in that frustration an occasion for truthfulness and even hope.'[56] We pay attention to the world in the light of the Gospel, and learn to work with what we find – not in the expectation of success, but doing what we can with what we have, responding in the language we are learning, open to learning more. We work not with resignation, but with patient hope, scraping away what we can of the tarnish that prevents the world around us reflecting God's glory.

It could even be said that contemplative pragmatism involves *detachment*, which, properly understood, is 'not a strategy of disengagement, but the condition for serious involvement with the world, unfettered from the fears and projections of the ego'.[57]

> Our *commitment* to the world is deepened, not diminished, by the capacity to live with detachment – that is, to live in the world in a way that does not constantly order the world around the pivotal points of my needs and my reactions. And if we can grow into commitments like this, our action for justice in society will be significantly different – capable of living with incompleteness and limitation, with an ambiguous world where solutions are not always to be had and never to be had swiftly and innocently; capable of living with silence, with something of the patience of Jesus, while living also with the *passion* of Jesus for the healing of the world.[58]

Most of all, contemplative pragmatism involves us in looking at ourselves and our world, 'long enough and hard enough for God to come to light', for

> our faith . . . depends on the possibility of meeting Christ in any and every place, and in any and every person. The degree to which we fail to find him, see or hear him, in anyone, is the

degree to which we have not grasped – or rather yielded to, been grasped by – his Lordship.[59]

Drawing on the language of some Welsh hymns, which see the landscape around them as the land in which God walks – the land of Emmanuel, *Tir Emanwel*, of God with us – Williams says:

> the Christian has to be aware that where he or she actually is is where God is to be found. This is the landscape of covenant, exodus, restoration. But this means that this is also the landscape of error, blindness, misrecognition. We walk on in the trust that a way can be found, and that at the end of the journey we shall find ourselves in a place from which the path will be clear as we look back. Meanwhile, we continue in the desert or the dark, repeating our faith that this and nothing other is in fact the land of promise. *Tir Emanwel* is here and now. The longest and hardest journey is the one to where we actually stand.[60]

Being an adult is, for Williams, not an arrival in some promised land of independence and control: it is this long, hard journey – a journey of patient contemplation, of fallible pragmatic action – a journey in hope, but a journey which will take us through the valley of the dark night's shadow. It is a journey along which we slowly discern who we are, and what our world is, and begin to sense the act of God running fiercely through all things.

IV

It is with this vision of adulthood in mind that Williams can turn his attention to childhood, and to the ways in which we prepare children for maturity. We live in a society, he believes, 'for which the education of children is essentially about pressing the child into adult or pseudo-adult roles as fast as possible'.[61] We assume 'that human beings do not have to *learn* to choose; will triumphs over the messy and time-consuming business of reflection, the thinking through of our relationships and dependencies'.[62] We ignore the fact that all choice involves consequences, involves the loss of other possibilities, involves responsibilities towards those affected by our choice – and that *learning* to choose requires a protected space in which children can play with and fantasize about choosing while preserved from the consequences of that choosing.

> Protecting the human young from some of the pressures of adult choice implies a recognition that such choice is weighty, potentially tragic, bound up with unseen futures for the agent and other agents. To learn about this . . . requires a space for fantasy, a licence for imagination, where gradually the consequences, the self-defining knots, of adult choice can be figured, fingered, experimented with.[63]

Protecting children from the pressures of adult choice involves concerning ourselves with the *integrity* of childhood – of play, of imagination, of experimentation; it involves our refusal to allow childhood to be 'colonized' by adulthood. Yet we live in a society where the space in which children might learn to choose is squeezed to make room for purely functional preparation for adulthood: a very different kind of learning.

Williams asks what our schools teach children – not so much by examining the curriculum, as by looking at the environment in which we teach and the ways in which we teach. What are we teaching children in schools where 'an anxious and overloaded timetable tells students that the fundamental requirement upon them is to *justify* their interests, projects and pursuits because of the scarcity and preciousness of time'?[64] What are we teaching children in a culture where their achievement is measured and tabulated at every turn, and the success or failure of the adults and institutions around them is made to rest on their results – an environment in which children are taught that value comes on numerical scales, and that life consists of the struggle to move up those scales? What are we teaching children in a world where language is dominated by 'the deadness of bureaucratic jargon, the deadness of uplifting waffle, the deadness of acronyms and target setting' rather than the development of resources for linguistic discrimination and expression, the developing of a resource for the patient exploration of the world, and 'for the extremities of experience, obsessive passion or jealousy, adoration, despair'?[65]

In ways like this, we are *all* involved in a failure to protect children. That failure is not simply 'a scandal caused always by someone else's failure, by people of extreme and pathological compulsion'; rather we need to ask 'how our whole life together as a society shows a level of emotional deprivation, an inability to become adult enough to care for our children' – the emotional deprivation shown fundamentally in our *impatience*.[66] And this impatience is compounded by the myths we spin of children's innocence, stories that absolve us from undertaking any kind of moral education – the beginning of that lifelong learning to look beyond the gratification of the self, beyond the ego's control. We race to teach children what they do not need, and neglect what they do need; we fit them for the market, but do not win them to the world of speech and interaction, of relationship and gift.

Williams believes that faith-based schools have something to offer in this situation. He has no patience with the claim that they somehow remove education from the public sphere and hide it behind the walls of religious ghettoes, furthering the fragmentation of our society. Quite the opposite, he says: if we exclude the possibility of faith schools, we further a separation of faith from the public sphere which weakens the commitment of faith communities to that public sphere – which ensures that their *real* teaching goes on behind closed doors, away from public conversational give and take. To allow the possibility of faith-based schools ensures that, for instance, Anglicans in Anglican schools will be forced

to defend and explain their ideas in the context of a wider critical world; they subject their teaching style and content, their religious education and moral ethos, to (literally) inspection.

They make the Church accountable in some significant ways. And by bringing the Church into this wider world, they make for a more not a less intelligent religious mentality.[67]

In return, Williams suggests, faith-based schools may have the resilience to offer something for which there might otherwise be no time and energy. He asks whether, precisely because they have access to a rich vision of adulthood as something other than successful consumerism, faith schools might have the resources to stand against the impatience which damages childhood, and prepares so badly for adulthood. He asks whether they can provide an environment which allows 'the formation of a free and critical mind – and an imaginatively generous heart'.[68] Can we prepare children not simply to consume but to contemplate? Can we prepare them not simply to will successfully, but to recognize the constraints and relationships which limit their wills? Can we, he asks, prepare children for adulthood?

V

Childhood and adulthood are both, for Williams, matters of learning – or, to use a word which has been much abused, of *spirituality*. They are stages on a journey into God, a journey towards our true selves, and towards open-eyed life in the world. To protect childhood and to foster real adulthood are not easy tasks: they require from us great patience and great vigilance. They require us to pay serious attention to what is taught in all aspects of our life together – our language, our environment, our practices, our rituals. The question which Williams forces us to ask in the Church is, 'What kind of people are we forming?' Are we in the Church learning together to live as finite creatures in God's world, alert for the kingfisher flash of God's brightness in things? Are we teaching patience, contemplation, pragmatism, relation? Are we teaching maturity – or are we keeping ourselves infantile, feeding adults sweets like children, and making children shoulder the burden of our infantilism?

As his comments on faith schools make clear, however, Williams believes that the questions of adulthood and childhood need to be posed to our wider society as well. When Pullman and others pose the question to the Church, Williams will – in his own way – join in; he will also, however, suggest that the Church has questions to pose to our culture. And once again, I suggest that it may be from this perhaps unexpected direction that Williams' impact might be felt politically and culturally during his tenure as Archbishop. Certainly he will have – as we shall see in the next chapter – things to say about peace and war, and about other controversial topics; it may be, though, that the most penetrating challenge which he might help the Church to bring to our world is the challenge to *grow up*.

Chapter Five

Politics and Peace

I

Imagine a large and diverse group of musicians finding themselves thrown together in a concert hall. One way in which they could organize themselves would be to scour the building for practice rooms, so that groups of musicians who happened to have the same instrument could practise together undisturbed by the others; the energy of organization would go into finding a large enough number of rooms, making sure that each of the rooms was well-enough soundproofed that the noise made in it need not disturb those in other rooms, and coping with the inevitable fragmentation when, for instance, the tenor saxophones decide that they want a room of their own, and do *not* wish to stay any longer with the alto saxophones – or when those violinists who have expensive instruments, instruments with a proper pedigree, decide they want a room away from the fiddlers.

Another way in which they might find themselves organized is if one set of musicians turn out to have especially loud voices: able to impose on the whole group their vision of what music should be played, and able to make sure that no musician or group of instruments is able to disrupt that vision. The only kind of music worth playing, they might say, is baroque chamber music – so I'm afraid that you drummers are going to have to play very, very quietly. And as for the trombones . . .

We might imagine, however, a different way forward – much more time-consuming, and much more difficult. We might imagine the musicians deciding to look for a way of making music together, a way in which they can make something which draws upon the possibilities of all the instruments present, but creates something coherent and sustainable. We might imagine them slowly, by improvisation, by careful and patient listening, and also by argument and negotiation and criticism, discovering ways in which the sound of each instrument could be a gift to the whole. It would be a process in which an alert ear would have to be kept open for attempts to dominate the music by any individual or group: attempts made by virtuosos to turn the whole into a concerto for their own instruments, and attempts made by others, less confident, to hide the sound of their instruments behind others. It would be a process in which no player or group of players ended up playing quite what she had imagined she would be playing; a process in which every player would find what they could play constrained by the necessity of blending with others – but it would also be a process in which ways would be found for each instrument to make a contribution to a whole which would not be itself without them. It would be a process which would require sensitive imagination: the kind of imagination that can hear, in the cacophony of a tuning orchestra, the possibility of the symphony that they might play.

It is in something like this vein that Williams can speak of a 'harmonic whole'[1] consisting of the 'free symphony of distinct wills'[2] or 'the polyphony of diverse created voices, human and non-human, reflecting back to God his own generous outpouring',[3] and asks us to 'think of the old-fashioned part-books, each singer being able to read his or her part only; so that the richness of the harmony will be new and astonishing to them'.[4] Musical metaphors provide him with a way of talking about the combination of distinct individuals into a whole which is more than the sum of its parts – which is neither simply a collection of those parts, nor the triumph of any individual part. They are metaphors which, in other words, help him to sketch a social vision which complements what he has said about adulthood – a vision which is neither libertarian nor authoritarian, neither liberal nor conservative. These musical metaphors are worth bearing in mind as we begin to explore the distinctive *political* vision which Williams' work contains: a vision, ultimately, of peace.

II

Implicit in much of what we have explored of Williams' theology so far is a vision of the human future – a vision of the future for which human beings were made, and towards which we are all called. Williams' vision is of a future fundamentally peaceful: a dance of unstinting giving and receiving. It is a biblical vision[5] – and it is a theological vision, which Williams took up from the Orthodox authors he studied at the start of his career, and made his own. It is a vision in which 'there is *one* human future',[6] a vision in which human beings, willy-nilly, belong together, and in which they are being drawn towards a future in which that belonging together becomes visible.

Williams' vision of the future which God has for the world is a vision centred on Christ: a vision of 'a single – or, better, a freely communicating – human culture, in which the diversity of human experience and human struggle would seem to be "at home" with, focused on, the identity of Jesus'.[7] It does not make Christian sense to think that 'becoming Christlike' means losing our differences, our particularities – becoming clones of Christ. To say that would be to assume that 'Christlikeness' was something which could be borne identically by individuals in very different situations, however different their backgrounds, however different their positions. And that would mean that 'Christlikeness' was something which could float above the messy involvements and relationships and histories in which we are involved: some kind of 'deportment' perhaps, which would carry us through those things unaffected. If 'Christlikeness' is that kind of characteristic, then it must be a characteristic that floats above Jesus' messy involvements and relationships and history too; it must be a characteristic which is only *illustrated* by Christ, but which could have been carried equally well by somebody else. And to say that would mean that, once we have grasped the point, once we have understood that free-floating characteristic, reference to the actual complex stuff of Jesus' humanity would become superfluous, even a distraction. He would remain useful as a sermon illustration, perhaps, but the detachable message which he brought would be the real heart of the Gospel, the real focus of faith.

As we have seen, Williams rejects this as a denial of the Incarnation. That doctrine tells us that it is Jesus in his particularity – Jesus as the particular human being he is – who is God's Word to us. He is not that Word despite being Jewish, despite being male, despite being from Nazareth, despite living in a particular time and place. He is God's Word precisely *as* that particular human being. He does not show us how life is lived fully for God *in general*, in a way which we could repeat identically – but shows us how life is lived fully for God by living his own particular life in unimpeded relation to God. If we are called to be Christlike, to share in Christ's movement towards the Father and his movement towards the world which the Father loves, then it is bound to be a call which we fulfil by looking different from Christ – by being drawn towards his Father and towards the world which the Father loves in our own particular time and place, in our own particular way, in relationship to Christ.[8]

If this is true, then the only way in which we learn fully what Christlikeness means is by seeing these particular lives – the life of Christ, and diverse other lives being shaped towards him – beside each other, mutually interpreting one another. We see a Francis of Assisi alongside Jesus, and are helped to see more of Jesus by the light we see in Francis' face and more of Francis by seeing him as a refraction of Jesus' light; and then we turn to a different face – a Dietrich Bonhoeffer, or a Thomas Merton, or a John of the Cross, or a Luther – and see Jesus differently, see more of Jesus, from their vantage. And then we turn to our neighbour and see him in the light of the Jesus we have learnt in all these other faces, and learn slowly to see what particular light this neighbour might himself throw upon Jesus. God, in drawing us into conformity to Christ,

wants particulars, not generalities. God does not, you might say, create clichés. What is bestowed on each of us is particularity, one utterly distinctive way of being Christ-like. If that one distinctive way of being Christ-like is frustrated or denied, then something in God's communication to the world is frustrated and denied. There is a sort of smudge across the revealed face of God.[9]

We *only* know Jesus fully – the Jesus of the Gospels, the Jesus who lived, died and rose again in a particular time and place – in the whole Body of Christ interpreting and refracting him down the centuries. Christ is not a principle – the sort of general lesson that could be repeated identically anywhere and every-where – but a person, and so the sort of reality which is explored fully only in the endless variety of particular relationships into which he enters.

It is the Spirit's work to conform us to Christ, making the light of Christ shine from our faces,[10] and that can *only* happen if the light of the glory of God in the face of Jesus Christ is refracted until it shines in a rainbow of differing faces.[11] There is no ten-sion between the diversifying work by which the Spirit fulfils each of us in our particularity, making us 'to be more, not less, ourselves',[12] and the unifying work by which the Spirit draws us into Christ. So, as well as being a vision of unity focused on Christ, Williams' vision of our common future is a vision of har-monious diversity animated by the Spirit – a diversity of gifts given by the Spirit for the building up of the whole. Williams writes about 'the Spirit as eschatological transformer of the cre-ated world'[13] who moulds and kneads us into what we will be, fitting us for our share in unfragmented communion.[14] It is the Spirit's work to make real the 'one human future' which is our inheritance and our promise, to make us 'members of the human race – no more and no less', by saving us from isolation and sepa-ration, and breaking us into openness and responsiveness to one another's differences. It is the Spirit's work to draw what might otherwise be a cacophonic disunity into symphony: to draw out each individual voice, and blend it into a greater whole. The Spirit's work is the work of *redemption*:[15] a work in which 'all the intractable, odd, baffling, resistant *singleness*' of each person is made into a gift to all.[16]

So, as we talk about the theological vision of peace which shapes Williams' thought, we are once again led into talking about the necessity of openness to other people who do not fit neatly into our schemes and priorities: who show us something *different*, something we could not have seen or said ourselves. Williams' vision of peace suggests that

> The stranger . . . is neither the failed or stupid native speaker, nor someone so terrifyingly alien that I cannot even entertain thought of learning from them. They represent the fact that I have growing to do, not necessarily into anything like an identity with them, but at least into a world where there may be more of a sense of its being a world we *share*.[17]

Faced with someone who does not simply replay to me the same old Christ I've already heard – who does not reflect to me Christ's light in precisely the colour I expect – I am called neither to condemn that difference as failure, nor to assume that they are reflecting a different Christ, but rather to explore patiently how it might be that the same Christ could be reflected from such different angles, in such different colours: to look for the Christ that we share, and so for the *world* that we share. And any challenges that we might make to one another, challenges to aspects of each of our reflections of Christ which can't be seen by the other as anything other than distortion, must emerge from such serious, generous and hopeful paying of attention.

In other words, when faced with your difference from me, the vision of ultimate peace does not call me to deny or break down that difference. Rather, it calls me to pay attention to

> your elusiveness, your mystery, your terrible singleness and solitude. And because your solitude, like mine, belongs to God, I shall stand before you as I stand before God. You are holy, as God is holy, and unknowable and unpredictable, as God is. So that I must give up and put away all hopes of trapping you in my words, my categories and my ideas, my plans and my solutions. I shall offer you whatever I have to offer, but

> I shall not commit the blasphemy (I don't use the word lightly) of ordering your life or writing your script.[18]

This is a vision for which *love* is fundamental.

> To purify love is to learn how egotistic fear and fiction work to smooth out the particular otherness of another person, so that my language remains uninterrupted, my control unchallenged, my involvement in time and chance unacknowledged. And to know this contingency in the event of love is precisely to retain and nurture an apprehension of the difference of this or that 'other', their own contingency; to be surprised, delighted, puzzled, hurt by them in a way which witnesses to their unassimilated reality, an independent hinterland to their side of the conversation.[19]

This is a vision which brings with it serious political consequences, because it implies a criticism of certain pervasive ways of looking at the present. It obviously undermines any view which sees us called to a uniform and unvarying sameness, any monochrome collectivism. But it also undermines any view which sees fragmentation as the deepest truth about human beings, any view which sees the world as *only* a contest between individuals with incompatible desires, incompatible 'goods'.[20] Williams does not, of course, deny the reality of contest and disunity; after all, it is part of being contingent, finite beings that we 'cannot guarantee the compatibility of goods', and part of being fallen that this contingency 'becomes meshed with rational beings' self-subverting choices of unreality over truth' so that 'the connectedness of human community becomes life-threatening as well as life-nurturing'.[21] Nevertheless, the theological vision of peace which shapes Williams' thought is a vision for which the tragic conflict of particular goods is not allowed to be humanity's ultimate truth,[22] 'atomic individualism' not our deepest reality. Any contest and conflict rests on top of a deeper unity, a unity given to us by God, and the Spirit's work is not to impose a false unity upon creatures who are *really* in conflict, but to make our true unity visible.

III

We have been talking about Williams' vision of the future set into orbit around Christ by the work of the Spirit, and we have been talking as if it were no problem to say that this is a future in which all people will be incorporated into the Body of Christ. Our language has oscillated between references to 'one human future' or 'the human race' and references to 'becoming Christ-like' or 'sharing in Christ's life'. There is a real and painful question as to how this vision might shape our action now in a world in which the centrality of Christ is far from transparent, and in a world in which the proclamation of that centrality would seem to be a move towards deeper contest and fragmentation: the raising of our voices in the shouted confrontation between different religions and worldviews.

The vision Williams has described certainly suggests that we can't simply rest content with religious isolation and disunity, with the Buddhists doing their Buddhist thing, the Muslims their Muslim thing, the Christians their Christian thing, and no concern for how we might find a world together. We can't rest content, we could say, simply with the hope that we will manage to find separate practice rooms for musicians with differing instruments. Any belief we might have had that such a resolution will make for peace should by now have been shattered by world events: the religions are all visions too comprehensive and too deeply ingrained to be restricted in this way; each implies commitments and desires which affect the way in which its adherents will behave in public, commitments and desires which affect the way they see the public realm and which therefore do not allow them to see secular arrangements simply as 'neutral'. The 'pluralist' solution, which seeks to preserve isolation and disunity and keep religion from distorting the public square is, in fact, one which stokes up violence: it arrogates to itself the chance to tell all religions (without any chance of negotiation or response) their limits, and so inevitably feeds – even creates – the sense that many religious people have that they are caught in a battle between their faith and the secular public square, fighting a rearguard action against secularity's advance. It allows religious people no way in which their faith can be brought with integrity to the negotiations and arguments of the public square, and so allows religious people to live out the public commitments they believe inherent in their faith only by means of one or other form of violence: whether it is the relatively benign violence which makes religions into pressure groups, fighting for particular public goals without their reasons for those goals being open to any kind of discussion or negotiation – or more malign forms of violence, of which we have seen far too many examples.

Williams' vision is clearly not one in which the religions can be kept in their own enclaves, free within them to do as they like, but allowed to claim no significance beyond them. It is a vision in which at least Christianity claims a wider significance than that – a universal significance. On the other hand, the character of the vision which Williams sketches is such that he can't simply see inter-religious relations in terms of a hope for everyone to leave behind their current identities and be turned into Christians – simply being subsumed into a finished and achieved identity, or handed a Christ whom Christians already possess.

On the one hand, then, Williams believes it to be Christians' vocation to bear the question which Christ poses anywhere and everywhere, and that means it is a question which we are to bear to those of other religions as well. And he can put this more robustly: Christians cannot do otherwise than approach inter-religious dialogue seeking for the formation of children of God after the likeness of Christ, and convinced that 'the stature of the fullness of Christ is what defines the most comprehensive future for humankind'.[23] Aware that this formation after the likeness of Christ will already be going on (the work of God being, of course, far, far wider than the Church), Christians will be ready to witness to Christ as a catalyst for, challenge to, affirmation of, and completion of that formation, inviting others to find in the stories of Jesus and the practice of Jesus' community, a vision which anchors the formation which is already taking place in them, and connects it with the formation going on in others.[24]

The vocation of Christians, Williams suggests, is to bear witness, to pose a question, and to offer a resource – and to do so across all boundaries, including across the boundaries dividing the religions.

On the other hand, Williams' is not a vision which allows us to think that we are possessors of an achieved and final truth which we simply need to *spread*, to distribute to others, so that the future could be the result simply of Christians 'winning' and everyone else 'losing'. It is of the very nature of his vision that it calls us to listening as well as acting, to discovering a way forward with others that we could not have invented on our own. As Williams says, 'a "theocratic" legal securing of the Christian vision' – i.e., our managing to secure the power and influence we needed in order to *impose* our vision upon others – 'would be a nonsense: it is worked out only in passionate and argumentative engagement in the uncertainties and limitations of human political action'.[25] But if this violent vision is a nonsense, it is just as much a nonsense to imagine a non-violent distribution of our achieved and secure position – so that we might hope to see the free and happy (and miraculous) adoption of *our* vision by everyone else, with no significant change occurring in the vision as it spread. To imagine that kind of future is still to imagine Christ as our possession – and that is not to imagine Christ at all.

The vocation of Christians is *not* to possess an overview, and it is *not* to stand immune from the challenges and questions and resources which others bring. Christians do not own Christ, and so cannot claim to know what will result when the question which Christ poses is heard and answered by others who differ from us. We cannot know in advance all that their 'formation after the likeness of Christ' might look like. In the process of encountering those of other faiths, and witnessing to Christ among them, we will find ourselves sent back to see Christ differently, to ask different questions – difficult questions, which shake what we have seen to be the 'obvious' ways of interpreting and following him. The process of 'mission' will involve *us* being questioned and challenged and shaken and changed – it will involve, we might say, *our* ongoing conversion.

Williams is painfully aware how difficult it is for Christians to bear the challenge of Christ to others with any integrity. He suggests, for instance, that the history of Christianity's relationship with Judaism means that 'Between the first century and the last few decades the idea of Christianity proffering to Judaism the crucified Christ as a challenge . . . would have been at best an ironic joke, at worst moral nonsense.' Christians are certainly unavoidably committed to the 'proclamation that Jesus is the embodiment of God's speech and purpose' in such a way as to put a question to Judaism – and Williams tentatively suggests that this challenge might, in Judaism's case, have something to do with 'the health and faithfulness of the chosen people, setting forth Jesus as a sign of the eschatological breaking of the boundaries of a people to create a new world for God'. But in the light of the very great evil of our dealings with Jews over the past two millennia, Judaism's 'resistance to absorption by the Church' is not just understandable, but vital. It witnesses precisely to Christians' all-too-common assumption that we *do* possess Christ, that we *do* possess an overview, and that we *do* therefore have the right to define others – and, in particular, to define Jews over against the Church as superseded, as old Israel, as those who have refused the Gospel, as those who killed the Messiah. Christians need to hear Jewish resistance to this attempt at a finalized overview – and need to see clearly something of the very great evil which such theology has allowed – in order to be called back to truthfulness and faithfulness. It may be that until we have heard that message, and learnt it more deeply than we seem to have done yet – heard and learnt from the witness which Judaism's resistance to Christianity has to offer us – there will be no way in which we can proclaim the Gospel with integrity among Jews: no way in which we can, in actual fact, function as bearers of the question of Jesus of Nazareth, rather than as bearers of the Church's diseased and life-threatening ideology.[26]

The Christian vocation, the pursuit of that vision in which we each become by the Spirit givers and receivers of Christ to those around us, can only proceed along such difficult routes – routes along which we receive as much as we give, routes along which we are convicted and converted again, routes along which we discover how little able we are to speak of Christ, still less to speak in Christ's name, to anyone. Williams remains convinced that encounter with Christ can and should transform any identity; he remains convinced that it is our vocation to proclaim Christ so as to allow that encounter to happen. But what it is to proclaim Christ's question to each other religion in this way needs to be patiently, humbly and carefully explored, and will be different in each case – just as, ultimately, what it is to bring Christ's question to each *individual* will be different. This difficulty and complexity must not reduce us to permanent silence, to the abandonment of the universal hope by which we live. All that we can do is throw ourselves into that process of questioning and counter-questioning, of paying attention with humility, and learning how to speak with integrity: discovering how to proclaim Christ without proclaiming ourselves. As those captivated by Christ, there is no alternative for us.

> We have something to say to human religiousness (our own included), but we are not in the business of winning arguments for good and all. What the world, religious and secular, does with the news of Jesus crucified and risen is beyond our control, and if it were otherwise we should have lost what our own 'news' is news of.[27]

IV

If we broaden our view from the inter-relation and co-existence of religions to the inter-relation and co-existence simply of people in general, we move decisively to the question of *politics*. The question of politics is, after all, 'How can we build a world together?' Williams asks of us, 'How can we participate in politics, in the building of a world together, in such a way as not to deny the Gospel? How can we participate in politics in such a way as to allow the Gospel to be audible?' It should be clear by now why he suggests that, to participate in politics in a Christian

way, we must act on the assumption that human beings fundamentally belong together, but also on the assumption that none
of us possesses an overview of the good to which we are called
together. We must act on the assumption that we can learn something from each other, and on the assumption that we all need
repeatedly to hear a challenge against our defensive egotism.

So, on the one hand, although we know ourselves to be caught
up in disagreements and negotiations and arguments, and know
those things to be important, we participate in them with the
knowledge that there is a more fundamental unity, a common
humanity, underlying those disagreements. Christians will believe
that we are *all* held in God's loving regard, and called to a common future, and that means that whether our negotiations
are successful or unsuccessful, whether our disagreements are
resolved or prove intractable, we simply can't dispense with one
another; we can't avoid one another. We have a *common* good,
whether we learn to recognize it or not. This belonging-together
provides the ground on which our negotiating and arguing can
go to work; it provides the territory which that negotiating and
arguing explore. If we are not to deny the Gospel, we must operate with the assumption that

> the basic human position is not that of individuals uneasily
> making treaties with each other, but of exchanges of recogni-
> tion, acknowledgements that within or alongside or against
> the world of calculated cooperation – and calculated non-
> cooperation – is a realm where the possibility and reality of
> exchange and common concern are agreed or given before-
> hand.[28]

On the other hand, although we know ourselves to have this
common ground, and so believe that we all truly belong together,
to be faithful to the Gospel we must so act as to acknowledge our
finitude and contingency – and that means acknowledging that
we work with limited perspectives.

It is simply not the case that we are able instantly to recognise and welcome an identity of interest in every other we come across. We are not transparent to each other in that way. We 'learn' each other, we cope with each other, in the trials and errors, the contests and treaties of speech; which takes time, and doesn't quickly or necessarily yield communion.[29]

Yet seen against the backdrop of the knowledge that we belong together – the knowledge of the unavoidable fact of our common humanity, our calling to a common end – politics is not simply the unending clash of opposing positions, or the attempt simply to minimize the violence of such unending clashes. It is a process of exploring ways in which we can discover together the common humanity which underlies those clashes; it is a process of bringing all of our limited perspectives, all of our partial understandings, together in order to seek the common good that might emerge from their interaction.

In other words, perhaps the most pervasive of Williams' political commitments is this commitment to *negotiation* in pursuit of *the common good*; his commitment to what he elsewhere calls 'the problem of restoring an authentically public discourse':[30] the attempt to find ways in which the players of all the different instruments can discover, by painful negotiation and by trial and error, how to play music together, how to *build* peace, on the assumption that peace is most fundamentally where they belong. We will not do this by stripping away all our differences to discover peace[31] but rather by finding a way to make our differences work together in the service of the 'free symphony of distinct wills'. We are called to discuss, argue, negotiate, explore; to criticize and accept criticism – to engage in the complex and messy business of strategy and settlement, the 'labour of public construction'.[32] And we are called to do this in pursuit of the common good.

This is a political vision which decisively pushes us beyond various existing forms of politics. It is, for instance, 'more than liberal'[33] – if the word 'liberal' is being used in its technical rather than a party political sense. 'Liberal' refers to a 'separate practice rooms' culture – a culture, that is, in which the rights of the individual are paramount, and society is seen as the playing field on which individuals negotiate, each seeking to be granted all to which he or she has a right. Of course, with scarcity of space and resources, it is not possible to meet everyone's rights all of the time, and so politics becomes the thankless art of trying to minimize the infringement of rights, and ensuring that no one group suffers an unfair share of the infringements. In liberal politics, individuals with rights are injured by the infringement of those rights; the healing of that injury can only come by reparation, the re-apportioning of some kind of property, which is bound in a situation of scarcity to infringe someone else's rights, and provoke inevitable counter-claims. The most that can be imagined in this kind of liberal politics is not peace, but an uneasy truce. However, for a more-than-liberal politics of negotiation towards the common good – a politics, we might say, of conversation – injury is not so much the infringement of an individual's or group's rights, but rather the breakdown in conversation between individuals or groups. The healing of such injuries is therefore not simply the attempt to fill up that individual's perceived lacks, but 'the creation [or re-creation] of some possibility of speaking together'.[34]

This vision of politics has important implications for *identity* politics: for the kind of politics which is focused, for instance, on the recovery of a 'black voice' in politics, or of a 'women's voice' – the giving of a voice in the political conversation to some group which has hitherto been denied a voice, or had imposed upon it a limiting voice in which it is only allowed to say things which chime with the wishes of those in power. That giving of voices, that discovery of voices, is vital, Williams says – and he agrees that the journey from having no voice to regaining a voice may be one which can only be achieved by robust self-assertion. Sometimes it is only by shouting that a group or a minority can become audible. Nevertheless, Williams understands the purpose of the rediscovery of such voices to be their joining in with the general public conversation by which we seek the common good. The end in view is not – to refer once more to the example with which I began – to provide a space in which a hitherto overlooked group of instruments can play their own music as loudly as they like without interference from anybody else. The end in view is rather the possibility that they will bring the distinctive contribution of their instruments to the construction of a common music – and that means to the give and take, the mutual qualification, the complex negotiation and conversation in which no voice can remain pure and strident, the expression of its owner's identity and nothing else, but in which all voices are constrained to discover a language in which they may speak so as to be understood by others, and responded to by others. If we wish to bring our voices to a common conversation, after all, then it will impose upon us a discipline:

> we cannot choose just any course of action in respect of our human and non-human environment and still expect to 'make sense' – that is, to be part of a serious human conversation in which our actions can be evaluated and thought through and drawn into some sort of rough coherence, by ourselves and by other speakers.[35]

'Identity politics' – the recovery and representation of silenced voices – is a vital move, but only a preliminary to serious conversation.[36]

Williams speaks in a similar vein about what liberation theologians have called God's 'option for the poor': God's standing on the side of those whose voices have been silenced. It is not, Williams says, that the owners of those voices, the 'poor', are morally superior. It is, rather, that God stands against our exclusion of the poor, against our refusal to allow them to participate fully in the construction of our world. The most important voices that we need to hear as we converse and debate in pursuit of a common good are precisely those voices that we have refused to hear, and those voices which we have forgotten how to hear; moves to allow those voices to hear are decisive moves in the direction of God's future. They do not, however, tell us what will happen when those voices are genuinely brought into the conversation, and become part of that slow, ongoing process by which we seek to find a world together. It is not that the voices of the poor are right about everything, not that their perspective is uniquely true – simply that they are *voices*, which we impoverish ourselves by neglecting.

Williams' politics is more-than-liberal, because it values bringing every voice to the table over giving every voice what it demands. Williams is nevertheless deeply concerned to avoid a 'corrupt appeal to social cohesion as an imperative that overrides the protests of a minority voice': his politics may not be 'liberal' as such, but it is certainly not 'authoritarian' or 'conservative' (again, in the technical rather than necessarily in the party-political sense). It is not a politics in which one group gets to set the music for all the others to play. He speaks of his vision as a search for 'civic vitality', the search for a life in common, a cohesive life; and notes that

> What I've called civic vitality actually assumes that such cohesion is *always in formation*: its shape is not yet given and could not be present in any sense without the release, the becoming audible, of all potential civic voices.[37]

After all, 'almost the only thing we can know about the good we are to seek is that it is no one's possession, the triumph of no party's interest'.[38]

> [W]e need to recover a politics, national and international, that insists on the primacy of questions about the corporate life we want and work for over questions of how we most successfully continue as we are.[39]

This non-conservative nature of Williams' vision becomes especially clear if we ask what role the Church might have in politics. The Church has often been seen (and often been seen accurately) as a force which stands overwhelmingly on the side of the preservation of the status quo. But if the Church is a place in which some vision like Williams' is sustained, it will necessarily be a place where the skill of seeing what contradicts this vision, what works against it, is nurtured. And the Gospel provides us with a resource for identifying what has been binding us to fragmentation and selfishness, and invites us constantly to go deeper into the work of naming and criticizing the arrangements and practices and habits that so bind us – calling us to pay serious, sustained, and critical attention to the society in which we live.[40] The Church is enabled to do this precisely because it believes in the Gospel – because it has a narrative which provides it with a vantage point from which to see differently.

> Political freedom has usually been understood as including some skills in questioning the options that are put in front of you by the system – the ability to imagine different futures. Such skills have everything to do with a lively sense of accumulated narrative, perspectives from elsewhere.[41]

The role which the Church plays is therefore primarily that of questioning – or of sustaining a vision of the future which brings with it questions.

> The church prays, the church studies, reflects, the church offers its worship, the church intercedes, and what's more, on the basis of all that, the church asks good questions, because out of this prayer and this worship the church gradually matures its sense of what a human being is like in such a way that it is equipped to ask awkward questions of the society around.[42]

One of the political roles of the Church, in fact, is to show that no arrangement of society, no current pattern, no habits and laws and customs, are unquestionable: 'the Church . . . is there to relativise all other belongings':[43] all must be brought to stand before the bar of the Gospel, and – thanks to the involvement of broken, distorted human beings like us – all of them will be found to be more or less inadequate. And so the role of the Church will not be inherently conservative, but rather inherently critical.

[T]he Church does not either affirm or deny 'the state' in the abstract: it asks what kind of humanity this or that state fosters – what degree of power in its citizens, what level of mutual care, what vision that is more than local, what scepticism about claims to absolute sovereignty and the right to absolute security. The Church does not either affirm or deny 'the nation' in the abstract: it asks whether or not people living with this or that corporate history, common language and culture, are capable of seeing it as a thread in a larger tapestry, or whether it is understood as something whose purity and survival are worth any price in blood and misery. And – a thought uncongenial, I know, to many British Christians – the Church does not either affirm or deny 'the family' in the abstract: it asks about the structures of material and psychological control in this or that family, about how the various patterns of family relation fail or succeed in creating creators of mutual relationship.[44]

V

'The Church does not either affirm or deny "the state" in the abstract.' It affirms it in so far as it provides an arena in which a conversation about the common good between differing interests can take place – an arena in which *politics*, in Williams' sense, can take place (which is not simply the same as providing a neutral arena within which competition between individual interests is regulated).[45] The Church cannot, however, regard the state as absolute or unquestionable: it can only see it as a provisional arrangement, a particular construction at a certain point of time, a contingent settlement, not a sacred given.[46] It has a vocation to contribute what it can to the reconciliation of human beings – by fostering conversation but also by resisting disorder and restraining mutual destructiveness. And this means that, as an entity whose deepest purpose is to promote reconciliation – to bring *all* into a conversation concerning the common good – it is *always* wrong for a state to kill, for killing is the final removal of a voice from that conversation. There may be times, Williams admits, when there is no alternative: when the only choice lies between greater and lesser evils, and the lesser evil involves the state in killing. But to accept that this tragic necessity has occurred and may occur again does not change the fact that killing denies the deepest purpose of the state; it does not absolve the Church from reminding the state of this purpose, and questioning its betrayal of that purpose. As a contingent reality with a purpose which it does not give itself but is given to it by God, and which it may therefore fulfil or betray to a greater or lesser extent, the state may be resisted when it distorts its purpose – and may be resisted when it claims to be more than a contingent reality, when it claims to be absolute, sacred, or unquestionable.

And so the state may not regard itself as having the right to survive at all costs. It is a contingent and limited reality, and is not itself the highest good but only one temporary way of serving that good, and that means that there are inevitably 'goods' that trump the good of the state's continued existence: there are ends that are worth more than the state, or evils it is more important to avoid than the destruction of a state. There must, for Christians, come a point when we are able to say, No, such and such a thing is not worth doing to preserve our security, because to do that thing would be to deny the good which the state exists to serve: it would be to choose endurance over integrity.[47] Williams refers us to the Old Testament prophets, who warn Israel against defending themselves by adopting the ways of the Gentiles: that would be to survive by losing the gift they had been given of a life of covenant with God; it would be killing themselves to survive.[48] And he refers to the remarkable discovery of Israel in exile: what they had been given, the life of covenant with God, survived the destruction of the nation which they had taken to be identical with that life. The good of the covenant is greater than the good of the nation, and the killing of the nation is not the same as the killing of the covenant. To have survived as a nation at all costs would have been to give up the life they had been given, to have endured only by turning their flesh into stone.

The more we seek, individually, socially and nationally, to

protect ourselves at all costs from intrusion, injury and loss . . .
the more we stand under Ezekiel's judgement for 'abominable
deeds' – the offering of fleshly persons on the altar of stone.[49]

And so, Williams says, nuclear weapons are absolutely and
unequivocally wrong. For a state to kill at all can only ever be
a tragic choosing of a lesser evil over a greater, and it is impossible to imagine a state faced with an evil which would make the
use of nuclear weapons a *lesser* evil. Nuclear weapons threaten
devastation on an unimaginable scale: the end of politics, the end
of conversation at the press of a button. That is not a price worth
paying for the survival of our state, or of any state. Writing in
the 1980s, before the fall of the Iron Curtain, it is quite clear to
Williams that it would be better to have Russia invade, better to
fall under Soviet control for years to come, than to embark upon
the mutually assured destruction of a nuclear war. To think that
our survival, the survival of our way of life, of our values, somehow outweighs the destruction of the vast majority of people on
all sides of the conflict is an utter nonsense – a blasphemy.

And he has no great respect for the argument that we have
nuclear weapons only in order to preserve the uneasy peace which
a near balance of abominable weaponry produces. There is no
point in having them unless we are, in the last resort, believed
to be prepared to use them; there is no way in which we will be
believed to be prepared to use them unless we are, in fact, actually
prepared to use them – prepared to imagine situations in which
we would use them. And so the possession of nuclear weapons
always rests upon the calculation that *some* set of circumstances
would make their use appropriate. And Williams argues again
and again that *no* set of circumstances – not even a counter-
strike once we have been attacked by others with such weapons
– makes such wanton, gratuitous, excessive, disproportionate
violence acceptable.

That nuclear weapons were not, in fact, used during the Cold
War is not an argument that sways him. If you have a child who,
in order to rescue his ball, has run across the road in traffic but
happens not to have been run over, you do not decide that run-

ning across the road in traffic is in fact a fine and acceptable strategy to pursue when retrieving a lost ball. That we survived without a nuclear war was an accident – and we came within inches of not surviving. It may be the case that no sensible person would ever press the button to launch a nuclear strike, but since when have we been in the hands of sensible people? In the first place, as we have said, the possession of such weapons only makes sense if one can imagine circumstances in which one *might* press that button – and in the second place it does not take much imagination to believe that, under stress, paranoid and defensive politicians (paranoid and defensive just like us) might start thinking differently about how bad the situation needed to be in which that button should be pressed. To allow the possession of nuclear weapons is to place a bizarre level of trust in fallible human beings.

In any case, Williams believes that the peace secured by the nuclear stand-off was in fact only secured by the siphoning off of conflict between the superpowers to the battlegrounds of countless developing countries – protecting our way of life at the expense of those whose voices we could not hear. The Cold War was not cold at all: it was fought in the heat of repeated bloody battles in African and Middle Eastern and East Asian countries; the security and peace of the superpowers was bought at the price of millions of lives, and the long-term destabilization of large portions of the world. Only now, perhaps, are we learning the price that the developed nations of the world might have to pay for decades of this strategy – as it turns out, predictably enough, that we are not immune from the violence which we tried to export.[50]

To blame this on politicians or presidents is, however, to miss the point. The preconditions for violence, for war, are laid precisely by our projection of our problems onto others; the interpersonal, national, and international are inseparable. We can't deal with the illusions and distortions which shape our foreign policy without at the same time dealing with the illusions and distortions in which we ourselves are caught up. 'I shall not truthfully see the web of lies in which our public life buzzes away,'

Williams says, 'until I have recognised where the fissures of the same untruthfulness run across my own moral vision.' Or, more pointedly: 'The decay of peace begins with me and you.'[51] It is we who desire to defend ourselves and our way of life at all costs; we who reinforced our sense of our own security by projecting our fears onto others, turning those who oppose us into monsters, imposing on them an identity designed simply to shore up our own. This is the common coin with which we conduct our lives in private and public, and so we should not be surprised when we discover that it is how we have allowed our world to work on the large scale. Our only way forward is not to proclaim ourselves righteous, unsullied by the moral grime which has coated our politicians and army chiefs – but to throw ourselves into the fragility and vulnerability of a conversation about the common good, into 'politics' in the broad sense. And that is true at the personal level, at the national level, and at the international level: there is no quick route from the mess we are in to moral purity. There is only, for us, the ambiguity of commitment to diplomacy, to negotiation, to give and take, conversation, debate, and argument. And there is no guarantee attached to any of that: no guarantee of success, no guarantee that it will not be swept away by the violence of one or other of the players, no guarantee that it is safe and secure. The future of harmonious unity is not one we can produce, but is one which we can only be given by God; we must in the meantime choose between the escalating demands of supposed guarantees of security – which eventually evacuate the life they are securing of all its positive content – and the dangerous and slow and ambiguous paths of politics. For Williams, the Christian vision of the human future allows us only one of those options.

Chapter Six

Sex and the Gospel

I

We are very good at letting ourselves off the hook. When we look for clear moral guidance, we often do so in part so that we do not have to *think* – so that we do not have to ponder our actions, or ask ourselves what they communicate. If we're following the rules, we think, we must be all right, so there is nothing further to be said. This is Atkins diet morality: we see ourselves as consumers faced with a supermarket shelf of possibilities; we check our rule book to see which ones we are not allowed, and then happily and without deliberation are able to do whatever we like with the items that remain. Unsurprisingly, Williams thinks that making moral decisions is a good deal more difficult than this.

> What we seek as we choose our path in life is what reflects the demands of the covenant, what is an appropriate response to the complete commitment of God to us. The Law tells me what kinds of action in themselves represent betrayal of God, but in deciding what, positively, I must do, I seek to show the character of God who has called me through my people and its history.[1]

'How can we so act as to *show* the character of God?' is a far more demanding question, and a far more open question, than 'Is this on the list of forbidden actions or not?' It is a question which demands of us not just knowledge (of what the law demands) but *wisdom*: the kind of responsiveness, discrimination and insight built up by slow, deep learning of the nature of God. Remember how, in his discussion of God's action, Williams argued that we should see God's acts not as the arbitrary and unquestionable decisions of an absolute will, but as expressions of God's nature – as ladders let down by God for us to climb further into his nature. When discussing *our* action, Williams has the same picture in mind: how can our actions reflect the journey into God to which we have been called? How can they pass on that summons to the heart of God to others? How can we become open to God's action, and to the opening up of God's life to others which is the purpose of God's action? How can I 'act in such a way that my action becomes something given into the life of the community and in such a way that what results is glory – the radiating, the visibility of God's beauty in the world'?[2] How can my acts be *gifts* which build up the life of Christ's body, which bear the question of Jesus of Nazareth in the world, which serve the Gospel?

These are not the kind of questions to which there exist quick answers; there are no general answers that will let us wriggle free from the hook of continual learning, continual questioning, continual readiness to repent. As I have stressed more than once, in Williams' theology the Spirit drawing us towards God in conformity to Christ does not impose uniformity upon us: the Spirit does not ignore or undo our particularity; in the Spirit's work we are made to be more fully ourselves. And that means that, finally, the question of how I am to act – how I am to display Christ, how I am to radiate God's glory, is one only I can answer. Making moral decisions cannot be, in this vision, simply about imposing uniform patterns upon everyone everywhere.

And yet Williams' view is certainly not that we may be indifferent to the views of others when we act. In learning how to act well, I ask myself, 'Can I so act as to make my action a gift to the Body of Christ?' Can I, that is, so act that my action becomes a lens through which others can see more of Christ, can be taken deeper into Christ? This is a question which forces us to consider not simply the discernment of individual Christians about what actions they should undertake, but the corporate discernment of the Body of Christ. To speak of making our action a gift to the Church – a gift which gives more of Christ to Christ's Body – inevitably forces us to ask how the more we seek to offer relates to what is already there. What is it for us to offer our action as a gift which gives more of Christ to the Body of Christ – a gift which speaks to the Body of Christ about the one whom they already know? What will it be, we must ask, for our actions to be *recognizable* as a gift by the Body of Christ?

In order to see what might be involved in answering these questions, Williams begins by approaching them from the other side, asking what it would be for him to recognize *others*' action as a gift to the Body of Christ in a case where he is not immediately convinced of the appropriateness of that action. He gives as his example his response to those Christians who have, after prayerful thought and careful deliberation, concluded that the possession of a nuclear deterrent is a tragic necessity, and one they are called upon as Christians to support. Williams, whose views on this I described in the last chapter, finds himself torn. On the one hand, the decision to support a nuclear deterrent is one which speaks an utterly foreign language to him – which he finds it all but impossible to recognize as a gift:

> I cannot at times believe that we are reading the same Bible; I cannot understand what it is that could conceivably speak of the nature of the Body of Christ in any defence of such a strategy . . . I cannot grasp how this reading of the Bible is possible; I want to go on arguing against it with all my powers, and I believe that Christian witness in the world is weakened by our failure to speak with one voice in this matter.[3]

On the other hand,

> these are people I meet at the Lord's table; I know they hear the scriptures I hear, and I am aware that they offer their discernment as a gift to the Body . . . I am forced to ask what there is in this position that I might recognise as a gift, as a showing of Christ.[4]

Struggling to be as open as he can to what this discernment might have to offer to the body, Williams recognizes that his opponents' stance

> reminds me that in a violent world the question of how we take responsibility for each other, how we avoid a bland and uncostly withdrawal from the realities of our environment, is not easily or quickly settled. In this argument, I hear something that I need to hear which, left to myself, I might not grasp.[5]

He can glimpse a dim flicker of gift in his opponents' action – but is forced to ask, is this enough? Is it enough to ameliorate his sense that they are speaking a wholly different language, and one which does not build up but destroys the Body of Christ? Should this be, for Williams, a point at which he finds himself out of communion with his opponents – a point at which he can no longer recognize that they are serving the same Christ?

The question which Williams faces at this point is not, therefore, 'Is it right or wrong to support nuclear weapons?' That is a question over which he is sure of his ground – a question on which he thinks the Gospel is quite clear: he remains convinced that those who support nuclear weapons are simply wrong, and he continues to feel called to fight against the views which his opponents propose. The question by which he is faced is rather the question of whether this is a disagreement deep enough that it should lead to the breaking of communion. And on this harder question he is 'left in perplexity'; he finds himself pushed to 'the edge of what I can make any sense of'. He also finds himself heir to a Christian tradition in which, from time to time, Christians have decided that they have reached a communion-dividing disagreement – being on occasion (Williams believes) quite right to do so. He refers to the response of Dietrich Bonhoeffer and others to the anti-Jewish legislation of the German Protestant churches under the Nazi regime – to Bonhoeffer's conviction that 'this so cut at the heart of any imaginable notion of what Christ's Body might mean that it could only be empty to pretend that the same faith was still shared'.[6] Williams is left to struggle with the question of whether he has reached a similar point, aware of the temptation to moral grandstanding, to serving his own ego by dramatizing an issue and striking the pose of a man of conscience; aware also of the temptation on the other side to choose polite and inoffensive unity, to let his action be dictated by a desire for a smooth ride – the temptation to forget that 'Unity at all costs is indeed not a Christian goal; Christian unity is "Christshaped" or it is empty.'[7]

The decision which he has evidently made to remain in communion with those who support nuclear weapons, is not – absolutely not – a decision to accept that they were right, or even a decision to accept that their position represents a possible interpretation of the Gospel. It is, rather, a decision to live with the brokenness within the Body of Christ which this disagreement brings. In part, to live with this brokenness means to 'sacrifice a straightforward confidence in our "purity"'.

> If I conclude that my Christian brother or sister is deeply and damagingly mistaken in their decisions, I accept for myself the brokenness in the Body that this entails. These are my wounds; just as the one who disagrees with me is wounded by what they consider my failure or even betrayal. So long as we still have a language in common . . . we have, I believe, to turn away from the temptation to seek the purity and assurance of a community speaking with only one voice and embrace the reality of living in a communion that is fallible and divided.[8]

'So long as we still have a language in common. . .': this decision to remain in communion in a broken body is founded on Williams' recognition that, in making their moral discernment, his opponents are struggling to be obedient to one who is *recognizably the same Lord* – and that is the only criterion which Williams has to offer us. There is no way, if Williams is right about the character of moral decision-making in the Church, that reading a few paragraphs can answer our moral dilemmas, or answer our questions about the making or breaking of communion for us. To discern how we should go forward, there is no alternative to a long process of careful listening, a renewed study of the Scriptures and the tradition, and painful self-examination – with the knowledge that, at the end, our decisions will only be a fragile and fallible venture, made without the support of absolute laws putting us clearly in the right or in the wrong. Nevertheless, Williams' discussion does make the *questions* clearer. The question we face when making moral decisions is, 'Can my action come to show Christ to others?' – and the question we face when asking whether our disagreements must break our communion is, 'Can I see that my opponents are making their decision in service to one who is recognizably the same Lord – recognizably the Jesus of the Gospel?'

II

The nature of these questions may become clearer if we turn to one particular moral issue which, for any reader who knows something about current debates in the Anglican Church, is bound to have been clearly in the background since this chapter began: sex. Williams' views on homosexuality, and their consequences for the Anglican Communion, have been much examined and debated, and I am not going to try here to give a comprehensive interpretation of those views, nor to plot how they fall on the spectrum of Christian opinion. I am simply going to set out two sides of Williams' contribution to this question: his suggestions about how in the realm of sexual relations I might look for ways of acting which show the character of the God who has called me; and his suggestions about how we might go about testing whether his views are gifts to the Body of Christ, or whether they are fatally community-dividing.

How might sexual activity show the character of God? How might it communicate Christ? Williams' analysis of sex is designed to answer precisely those questions. He begins by asking, What happens when I desire someone?[9] I see someone and I desire them: I perceive that person as an *object* of desire – but that in itself is not enough. If my desire is to be fulfilled, the other person has to recognize that I desire them, and has to welcome that desire and desire me in return: otherwise I'm left just looking – or, worse, am rejected. So I have both to see the person I desire as an *object* of my desire, and see him or her as a *subject* who desires *me*. And that in turn means that I also have to see *myself* as the object of his or her desire. (This may sound complicated, but think of someone who cannot imagine themselves as in any way desirable; surely that would stand in the way of entering a properly mutual relationship?)[10]

Now, our initial desire for the other person might be thought of as a straightforward biological drive – and it is certainly not a purely cerebral reality, but something in which my whole body is involved – but these other perceptions (of the desired person as one who desires me, and of myself as desired by him or her) are more complex and subtle; they are matters of interpretation, of *reading* the other person, and of learning to *understand* myself in a new way. And because it involves 'reading' the other person and 'reading' myself, because it involves mutual interpretation, Williams can speak of such desire as involving 'language' – not in the sense that it has to involve speaking or writing, but in the sense that it has to involve *making sense* – making sense of someone else, and making sense of myself. (Think of someone who has fallen in love, trying desperately to read all the signals she receives from her beloved: Does he like me? Did his glance mean anything? Did he deliberately choose to sit next to me? – all of these are attempts to learn the language which the beloved's actions speak.)

And Williams claims that this 'reading' and 'speaking' necessarily involve *vulnerability*.[11] They involve both allowing my desire to be seen by the other person – allowing the other person to 'make sense' of me, allowing the other person to understand that I desire her, and so risking her rejection – and they involve my reading her as potentially responsive, or already responding; they involve my risking an interpretation of her. And so, as Williams says, 'All this means . . . that . . . I am no longer in charge.'[12] It means being handed over into someone else's hands, becoming dependent upon that other person: the fulfilment of my desire depends on becoming available as the fulfilment of the other person's desire; seeking my own joy is only possible by seeking the other person's joy.

And it is because of this that Williams can say that, for many of us, 'sexual intimacy . . . is quite simply the place where [we] begin to be taught whatever maturity [we] have'.[13] In other words, for many of us it is in a sexually intimate relationship more, perhaps, than anywhere else – precisely because they can be relationships in which we are more fully exposed – that we can learn how vulnerable we are to another, how dependent we are upon another, how destructive our defensiveness is, how damaging our attempts to protect ourselves from all our dependence upon our partner or our partner's dependence on us.

Sex is – or at least can be – about mutual vulnerability, about being exposed to another, about being placed into another's hands metaphorically as well as literally; it is about no longer being able to protect and secure my ego behind its own walls; it is about discovering the helplessness of the ego, and being pulled out of being centred entirely on myself. And at the same time it is about discovering ourselves as desired, as desirable, as loved and held – and as being given the gift of another person's vulnerability, another person's exposure, so that we have that other person in our hands. Or that, at least, is an account of what *can* be good about sex: a good which is much deeper than simple 'pleasure', and which is distinct from the good of reproduction. Sex can be, Williams is suggesting, something which reflects and draws us into the self-giving vulnerability of love, which mirrors the life of God.[14]

Even in this unpromising world, where we are so prone to deceive ourselves, things and persons can come to 'mean', to show, God's meanings – to communicate the creative generosity and compassion which, we learn from revelation, is the most basic reality there is . . . [and] sexual love becomes sacramental when it involves a lasting . . . resignation of control, a yielding to the other, a putting your own body at the disposal of another for that other's life and joy.[15]

It is only once Williams believes he has at least a provisional account of how sexual relationships can be an aspect of our humanity which can be made to speak of Christ that he can go on to start talking about what can be bad about sex, how sexual relationships might fail to speak of Christ, or might speak of Christ untruthfully. It is precisely because he has an account of sexual intimacy's tremendous power for good that he can begin to think through what the distortion and misuse of that power might look like – and so begin to speak about 'failure', 'immaturity', and 'perversion'.[16]

In other words, Williams' attempt to understand sex as good certainly does not mean that he thinks 'anything goes'. As we shall see in a moment, he is quite prepared to condemn some forms of sexual relationship – even some forms which have often been found perfectly acceptable. His understanding of good sex gives him, as a mirror image, a concept of bad sex – sex that instead of opening us up to the other, instead of encouraging vulnerable growth, locks us more deeply into ourselves. A sexual encounter in which the other is reduced to an object, simply becoming material for my gratification, is one in which there is no exposure to the partner's desires and perceptions, no vulnerability; such sex is a distortion and a perversion. That is most obviously the case in rape, in paedophilia, and in bestiality – activities in which the other person is disregarded as a person for the sake of my gratification, and in which I refuse all vulnerability myself and make the other the vulnerable one – and these are terrible and damaging distortions of the 'good' that sex can be. But Williams goes further than that in exposing bad forms of sexual relationship. Far from having a laissez-faire attitude to sex, he is concerned that we sometimes let ourselves off the hook far too easily. We say, 'Sex within marriage is good, sex outside is bad' – and think that this means we no longer have to think about marital sex morally, or theologically. But actually, sex *within* marriage can be pretty bad in the sense we've been talking about. Marital sex can be bad, for instance, if it is seen as a right of the husband to gratify his desires using his wife, whether or not she's willing. And that, or something like it, has been how marriage has been seen in many cultures and periods of history – how it is all too often still seen in our own culture and time – so Williams can make what he calls a 'perfectly serious suggestion' that 'in a great many cultural settings, the socially licensed norm of heterosexual intercourse is a "perversion"'.[17] It is, in other words, a deep, deep distortion to think that what is right and wrong in sex is a matter of what feeds *me*; or even that what is right and wrong in sex is a matter of 'doing no harm'. As Williams says 'both of those responses are really to give up on the human seriousness of all this' – they are refusals to think seriously about vulnerability, mutual openness, and risk.

Williams goes on to recognize the difficulty, and sometimes the absurdity, of sexual relationships – the difficulty and potential absurdity that are built in to any activity in which we become so vulnerable. Sex, as he has repeatedly said, is a risky business, and good sex in Williams' sense needs a context in which taking risks together, and risking ourselves with each other, is possible. 'Sexual faithfulness is not', he says, 'an avoidance of risk';[18] it is the proper context for risks so deep. In a review of a book by Elizabeth Stuart he expressed extreme scepticism about her suggestion that we might, as reasonable adults, be able to negotiate non-monogamous sexual relations within the context of a network of friendships – this ignores, he says, the seriousness of the passion and commitment, and of the related opportunities for self-deceit and betrayal.[19] Such possibilities and such dangers require immense commitment, time, and openness.

So Williams believes that his vision of the good of sex leads him to affirm that sex is properly explored within faithful, publicly committed relationships:

> I believe that the promise of faithfulness, the giving of unlimited time to each other, remains central for understanding the full 'resourcefulness' and grace of sexual union. I simply don't think we'd grasp all that was involved in the mutual transformation of sexually linked persons without the reality of unconditional public commitments: more perilous, more demanding, more promising.[20]

'I have always been committed', he says, 'to the Church's traditional teaching on sex before marriage and adultery!'

> It seems to me obvious that if we are to show God's costly commitment in all areas of our lives, this applies here as elsewhere. We may want to be compassionate and realistic with people coming from a setting where these ideals are remote or completely unintelligible – but the last thing I'd want to do is to weaken the challenge and excitement of that traditional view that says we can and should demonstrate God's faithfulness in our bodily lives, and that this is the meaning of Christian marriage.[21]

When it works, 'marriage is about more than just stability; it's about the risk of passionate engagement – wanting the fellowship of another so deeply that you mortgage your own abstract freedom by a rash public promise intended for life'.[22] As such it is a school of commitment and passion which is the best context for the nurturing of children who need to grow into committed and passionate adults. 'Marriage matters', Williams says, 'because of this evoking of gift and risk and mutual joy, because this is the very heart of what we believe about our God and how he works with us.'[23]

On the other hand, Williams insists that we can't simply say that *everything* about all other forms of sex is bad. Just as we can't simply say that everything in here (inside fully committed relationships) is good and only good, so we can't say that everything else, everything out there, is bad and only bad. There may well be glints and gleams and seams of what is good about sex even in the midst of inadequate, immature, distorted, and bad forms of sexual relationship: 'an absolute declaration that every sexual partnership must conform to the pattern of commitment or else have the nature of sin *and nothing else* is unreal and silly'.[24] And that means not that the Church should give up on its commitment to faithful monogamous marriage, but that when we encounter those who have had or are having kinds of sexual relationship which differ from the publicly committed, long-term, mutually vulnerable form which the Church holds out as 'good', we do not always have to say 'Everything about what you've done or are doing is wholly bad and needs to be absolutely denied.' Rather, we can say, 'Look, there is a fuller good towards which anything good in what you've been doing points – a deeper, more challenging, more promising good which can transform and complete the good you have experienced.'

Williams suggests that the way he has been identifying the 'good' of sex means we can at least think about sex as good without having to think about it as tied to procreation – and he argues that that is a claim which has strong biblical backing. However, he goes on to make the more controversial statement that, in the light of this, he can see no bars to the affirmation of long-term committed same-sex relationships. He argues that he can't find reasons *built in to the Gospel*, built in to the Christian under-standing of creation and redemption, for rejecting all homo-sexual sexual activity as necessarily 'perverse' in the sense he has defined. He would need *further* reasons, different reasons, to make that rejection – and he thinks the 'further reasons' on offer are inadequate: the 'deployment of a number of very ambigu-ous texts, or . . . a problematic and nonscriptural theory about natural complementarity'.[25]

He looks, for instance, at the text in Romans 1 which many take to be the decisive biblical reference to homosexuality. That text, he argues, defines its object as 'the blind abandonment of what is natural and at some level known to be so, and the deliber-ate turning in rapacity to others', and he suggests this might not be a good description of what takes place in those committed long-term, faithful, sexual relationships which explore the same passionate vulnerability and self-sacrificing openness that he has been describing. He asks us to imagine a Christian homosexual saying 'I truly, prayerfully, and conscientiously do not recog-nise Romans 1 as describing what I am or what I want'[26] – and suggests that therefore a homosexual relationship might be one which instead of inherently obstructing the Christlike develop-ment of those involved in it, can, like a heterosexual relationship, show Christ to the world.

The heart of Williams' argument about homosexuality, then, is an attempt to look at sex in the light of the Gospel, and to understand how sexual relationships might be part of lives being caught up by the Spirit into God's life. That provides him with a biblical and theological basis on which to begin asking what kinds of sexual practices are in line with the Gospel, and what kind of sexual practices are wrong. Most of his conclusions are fully in line with traditional teaching, but he acknowledges that on homosexuality his attempts to understand the implications of the Gospel do not lead him to 'reaffirm the Church's historical position'[27] – but rather push him towards understanding the relevant biblical texts not as blanket condemnations of everything which we would think of as homosexual practice, but as making Gospel sense only when they are seen as condemnations of certain kinds of 'rapacious' homosexual behaviour. The weight of his argument does not fall on his analysis of Romans 1 or of texts like it: he undertakes that analysis only in the wake of his attempt to bring the *core* of the biblical witness – the Gospel of God's disarming acceptance – to bear on his understanding of sex. So, his reading of Romans 1 and similar texts is not unimportant, but it is secondary – and has to be seen in the light of his commitment to a Gospel-centred or Christ-centred reading of Scripture in general, which I discussed in Chapter Three. And so he can claim with some force not to be one of those for whom

the casting off of 'traditional' or even scriptural norms to do with certain kinds of sexual behaviour is part of a general programme of emancipation from the constraints of what they conceive to be orthodoxy, part of a package that might include a wide-ranging relativism, pluralism in respect of other faiths, agnosticism about various aspects of doctrine or biblical narrative, and so on.[28]

His controversial opinion on homosexuality, right or wrong, emerges for him not as an exception to or an amelioration of his attempt to be obedient to Christ, but as an example of it: an example of his attempt to analyse moral questions in the terms of the Gospel, and to ask what it is for us in our lives to manifest Christ to the world.

III

Williams knows, of course, that many will disagree with his particular conclusions on this matter. He asks those who disagree, however, to consider whether their disagreement is of the kind which should break communion – whether, in the terms we used earlier, it is a view which they can in no way recognize as a gift to the Body of Christ. Someone who disagreed with Williams might argue against his exegesis of particular biblical texts; he or she might, more pertinently, argue against the way Williams' theology describes the use of biblical texts in general; he or she might, more pertinently still, argue against the particular ways in which Williams understands sexual relationships in the light of the Gospel. All this is possible and, in fact, inevitable – and all of it could take place *within* a communion, *within* the Body of Christ. That isn't to say that disagreement about his particular conclusions – the kind of disagreement that is not necessarily communion-dividing – can't be very serious. It may be disagreement about matters that deeply wound the Body (as Williams believes the Body is wounded by a Christian commitment to nuclear weapons). But the seriousness of this wounding is contained within a wider coherence.[29] It may even be that the continued existence of such a disagreement can itself be turned to some good by the Spirit, who works through our fallibility and weakness. Speaking about a very different but no less divisive debate, that between those who accept and those who deny the propriety of baptizing of infants, Williams says,

> I don't know that we are ever going to get those views together, but we might at least begin to think out what it means that God has raised each of us up to say to the other something that the other can't say for him or herself, to remind us of what it is about our practice and our language that still does not get hold of the whole mystery.[30]

The *communion-dividing* question is different. To decide on whether this disagreement is communion-dividing, Williams suggests, is for each side in the debate to ask whether those on the other side can any longer be recognized as struggling to be obedient to the same Gospel, the same Christ. The disagreement would be communion-dividing, for instance, if his opponents became convinced that there was no way in which Williams' views could be described as an attempt to analyse moral questions in the terms of the Gospel, no way in which they could agree that he was asking what it is for us in our lives to manifest Christ to the world – or at least no way in which his views could be so described without the meaning of the words 'Gospel' and 'Christ' becoming utterly unrecognizable to them.

When the primates of the Anglican Communion met in Oporto in Portugal in 2000, they issued a 'Communiqué' which touched on the question of homosexuality – and which some thought a classic Anglican 'fudge' of the issue. The heart of that Communiqué, though, is no fudge but a set of statements which address precisely the kinds of questions which Williams suggests we need to address if we are to decide whether our differences divide the communion: questions that go deeper, that are more closely connected to the Gospel, than our particular disagreements about sexuality. These statements provide a proper context for our particular disagreements over sexuality to be hammered out. Having briefly sketched differing views on homosexuality, the Communiqué runs:

> We recognise the seriousness and sincerity behind both concerns, and the shared desire to be faithful to scripture and to strengthen our unity in Christ. We believe that our call to faithfulness and unity makes demands on our life of interdependence in several ways: We expect to see in one another a worshipping life, gratefully celebrating the sacraments given by the Lord Jesus and publicly proclaiming the Word of God in scripture; We expect to see a passion to share the unique Good News of Jesus Christ; We expect that, as we experience this worshipping life, we shall gratefully learn from each other

aspects of the riches of Jesus Christ that no one local church could learn for itself in isolation; We also expect that, when we see in each other what we believe to be failure or unfaithfulness, there will be freedom for plain speaking and 'fraternal rebuke' (Matt. 18.15ff.; cf. Gal. 2.11; Eph. 4.25). We expect honesty and challenge from each other. But we also look for humility, self-examination and a willingness to preserve those bonds of communion that reflect the unity we share.

Within our ministry to each other and our learning from one another challenge and disagreement are not only made possible but can be life-giving because of our commitment to one another in the family of the Communion. As in any family, the assurance of love allows boldness of speech. We are conscious that we all stand together at the foot of the Cross of Jesus Christ, so we know that to turn away from each other would be to turn away from the Cross.

It is deeply difficult to balance the expectation of learning from each other with the expectation of honest challenge. But we recognise the freedom to call one another to account in the name of the Lord. This clearly poses the question of what would be sufficient grounds for a complete and definitive rupture of communion between Provinces in the Anglican family. We recognise that one Province's adoption of certain policies may result in severely impaired communion with some other Provinces or dioceses (as has already happened in relation to the ordination of women). We believe that the unity of the Communion as a whole still rests on the Lambeth Quadrilateral: the Holy Scriptures as the rule and standard of faith; the creeds of the undivided Church; the two Sacraments ordained by Christ himself and the historic episcopate. Only a formal and public repudiation of this would place a diocese or Province outside the Anglican Communion.[31]

There is one last qualification to make here. As Archbishop of Canterbury, Williams does not believe that his 'first task is to fight for the victory of [his] personal judgements as if those were final or infallible';[32] or that he has been 'elected to fulfil a programme or manifesto of his own devising'.[33] Rather, his role is primarily to sustain the conversation: to work to ensure that each side can see what of commitment to the Gospel and of obedience to Christ there is in the other sides.[34] It is a role which involves a certain degree of stepping back from the debates that threaten to divide us, in the attempt to see and to help others see the common ground on which those debates take place – always at the risk of being thought by one side or another, or by all sides, not to be taking a firm enough line, or to be allowing conscience to be dented by expediency. It is a role which involves focusing squarely on what is most important, the Gospel of Jesus Christ crucified and risen, the Gospel of God's disarming acceptance, and drawing all sides in these debates to keep their focus on that Gospel firm.

Although sexuality is far from being the most important or interesting topic in his theology, this attempt to hold the debate to the Gospel – to keep the disputants at the foot of the cross – may prove to be the real test of Williams' ministry (although, of course, it is a test in which 'success' is not in his hands). And this is what those commentators miss who wish that Williams would have what they see as the moral courage to champion his own particular views on sexuality. Such a championing would, in fact, be a betrayal of his deepest commitments. We will have to wait to discover whether something of Williams' vision of a communal life of giving and receiving, of showing Christ to one another, of deepening encounter with the disarming acceptance of God, proves to be a captivating resource for the Anglican communion and others: a resource for the renewal of vision, and of the strengthening of bonds which are deeper than our controversies. We will have to see whether he continues to be treated by his supporters as a theological virtuoso, playing fascinating tunes which the rest of us could not hope to emulate, and by his opponents as a dangerous liberal, sitting light to the Scriptures – or whether instead his theology will prove open and inviting enough to encourage others in and beyond the Communion to join him in an ongoing conversation which explores ever more deeply the heart of God.

IV

It would be a pity to finish our exploration of Williams' theology with a discussion of sex, and of the controversy which it provokes. It is a topic which is all too likely to distract us from the heart of his message. Far better to concentrate on his vision of the fierce love of God, upholding the world and surging through all created things: the love visible in the face of Christ crucified and risen, the love which calls us to unending growth in gratitude and in openness to judgement, as the Spirit shapes us into Christ-like movement to the Father. Far better to listen with him to the swelling music of God's threefold life, played out to us clearly in the life, death, and resurrection of Jesus of Nazareth and now caught up and echoed back with deepening richness in the bodies of those who are being mastered by it, whose weak, fallible, mortal lives are being scraped clean and tuned so as to vibrate to its frequencies. This is, as we have seen, a demanding vision – a difficult Gospel – but it is one which has the capacity to re-awaken us to the central mysteries of the Christian faith. We may still pray and hope that, by the grace of God, such re-awakening will be the lasting legacy of Williams' theology.

Notes

Introduction

1 *OCT*, p. 270.
2 *A*, p. 236.
3 'Teaching the truth', in Jeffrey John (ed.), *Living Tradition: Affirming Catholicism in the Anglican Church* (London: DLT, 1991), pp. 29–43: pp. 33–5.
4 Review of Edith Wyschogrod, *Saints and Postmodernism* in *Modern Theology* 8.3 (July 1992), pp. 305–7: p. 307.
5 'Doctrinal criticism: some questions', in Sarah Coakley and David A. Pailin (eds), *The Making and Remaking of Christian Doctrine: Essays in Honour of Maurice Wiles* (Oxford: Clarendon, 1993), pp. 239–64: p. 240.
6 'Telling the Christmas story like it is', *The Guardian*, 23 December 2000.
7 'Teaching the truth', pp. 40–1.
8 Williams was arrested in 1985, having broken in to an American airbase to sing psalms in protest on the runway.
9 '"Religious realism": on not quite agreeing with Don Cupitt', *Modern Theology* 1.1 (October 1984), pp. 3–24; my italics.
10 'No life here – no joy, terror or tears', *Church Times*, 17 July 1998; Review of Hans Urs von Balthasar, *Engagement with God*, in *Downside Review* 94 (April 1976), pp. 153–4: p. 153.
11 *OCT*, p. xvi.
12 'Theology and the churches', in Robin Gill and Lorna Kendall (eds), *Michael Ramsey as Theologian* (London: DLT, 1995), pp. 9–28: pp. 22–4.
13 *OCT*, pp. xiii–xv.
14 *OCT*, p. 196.
15 Don Cupitt, in Michael De-La-Noy, *Michael Ramsey: A Portrait* (London: HarperCollins, 1990), p. 99; quoted in 'Theology and the churches', p. 9.
16 'Theology and the churches', pp. 19, 24.
17 *OCT*, p. 6.

1   *Disarming Acceptance*

1   The story of Jacob's return is told in Genesis 32 and 33.
2   'To give and not to count the cost: A sermon preached at Mirfield in February 1976', *Sobornost: The Journal of the Fellowship of St Alban and St Sergius* 7.5 (Summer 1977), pp. 401–3: p. 402.
3   *TG*, p. 26.
4   'The ethics of SDI', in Richard J. Bauckham and R. John Elford (eds), *The Nuclear Weapons Debate: Theological and Ethical Issues* (London: SCM Press, 1989), pp. 162–74: p. 171.
5   *TG*, p. 17.
6   *PTT*, p. 33.
7   *R*, p. 54.
8   *WK*, p. 1.
9   *R*, p. 54.
10 Jubilee sermon, Bangor Cathedral, 11 June 2002, <http://www.churchinwales.org.uk/archbishop/0015e.html>.
11 Matt. 8.20.
12 *R*, p. xii.
13 *R*, p. 30.
14 'Balthasar and Rahner', in John Riches (ed.), *The Analogy of Beauty* (Edinburgh: T&T Clark, 1986), pp. 11–34: p. 34.
15 John 1.14.
16 *OCT*, p. 21.
17 'Doctrinal criticism: some questions', in Sarah Coakley and David A. Pailin (eds), *The Making and Remaking of Christian Doctrine: Essays in Honour of Maurice Wiles* (Oxford: Clarendon, 1993), pp. 239–64: p. 257.
18 *WK*, p. 1.
19 *DL*, pp. 4–5, Williams' italics.
20 *R*, p. 83.
21 *DL*, pp. 6–7.
22 *DL*, pp. 6–7.
23 *OTJ*, p. 70.
24 *WK*, p. 5.
25 *R*, p. 86.
26 *A*, p. 239.
27 *R*, p. 55, Williams' italics.
28 *OCT*, pp. 159–60.
29 'Jesus – God with us' (with Richard Bauckham), in Christina Baxter (ed.), *Stepping Stones: Joint Essays on Anglican Catholic and Evangelical Unity* (London: Hodder & Stoughton, 1987) pp. 21–41: p. 28.
30 'A history of faith in Jesus', in Marcus Bockmuehl (ed.), *Cambridge Companion to Jesus* (Cambridge: CUP, 2001), pp. 220–36: p. 220.

31 *R*, p. 82.
32 *R*, p. 76.
33 *OTJ*, p. 131.
34 'The Lambeth Talk' (interview, Greenbelt Festival 2000) <http://www.
    fish.co.uk/news/ religion/rowan.html>.
35 *R*, pp. 71–2, emphasis removed.
36 *R*, p. 72.
37 Enthronement sermon, 27 February 2003 <http://www.archbishopof
    canterbury.org/sermons_speeches/>.
38 *WK*, p. 70.
39 *OCT*, p. 94.
40 Enthronement sermon.
41 *OCT*, p. 91, my italics.
42 'The ethics of SDI', p. 170.
43 'To give and not to count the cost', p. 401.
44 'Bread in the wilderness: the monastic ideal in Thomas Merton and Paul
    Evdokimov', in M. Basil Pennington (ed.), *One Yet Two* (Kalamazoo,
    Mich.: Cistercian Publications, 1976), pp. 452–73: p. 463, emphasis
    removed.
45 *OCT*, p. 159.

2   *The Source of Life*

1 Sermon at Canterbury Cathedral, morning service, 2 March 2003
   <http://www.archbishopofcanterbury.org/sermons_speeches/>.
2 *Eucharistic Sacrifice: The Roots of a Metaphor*, Grove Liturgical Study
   no. 31 (Bramcote, Notts: Grove Books, 1982), p. 30.
3 Presidential Address, 20 Sep 2001 <http://www.churchinwales.org.uk/
   archbishop/0011e.html>.
4 'Hooker: philosopher, Anglican, contemporary', in Arthur McGrade
   (ed.), *Richard Hooker and the Construction of Christian Community*
   (Washington, and Tempe, Ariz.: Centre for Medieval and Renaissance
   Studies, 1997) pp. 369–83: p. 371.
5 'Hooker: philosopher, Anglican, contemporary', pp. 372–3.
6 See *TVNL*; also 'The philosophical structures of Palamism', *Eastern
   Churches Review* 9.1–2 (1977), pp. 27–44; and 'The theology of
   personhood: a study of the thought of Christos Yannaras', *Sobornost:
   The Journal of the Fellowship of St Alban and St Sergius* 6.6 (Winter
   1972), pp. 415–30: p. 424.
7 *A*, p. 242.
8 *WK*, p. 51, emphasis changed.
9 Sermon at Canterbury Cathedral, diocesan service, 2 March 2003
   <http://www.archbishopofcanterbury.org/sermons_speeches/>.
10 *A*, p. 267.

11 A, p. 267.

12 A, p. 267.

13 'The Nicene heritage', in James M. Byrne (ed.), *Christian Understanding of God Today: Theological Colloquium on the Occasion of the 400th Anniversary of the Foundation of Trinity College, Dublin* (Dublin: Columba, 1993), pp. 45–8: p. 45, my emphasis.

14 OCT, p. 249.

15 PTT, p. 27.

16 PTT, p. 28.

17 'Reply: redeeming sorrows', in D. Z. Phillips (ed.), *Religion and Morality* (New York: St Martin's Press, 1996), pp. 132–48: p. 144.

18 TVNL, p. 65.

19 TVNL, p. 85.

20 WK, p. 58, Williams' italics.

21 OCT, pp. 183–96.

22 OCT, p. 192.

23 OCT, p. 194.

24 OTJ, p. 34, Williams' italics.

25 OTJ, pp. 34–5.

26 'Telling the Christmas story like it is', *The Guardian*, 23 December 2000.

27 OTJ, p. 10.

28 WK, p. 149.

29 'The necessary non–existence of God', in Richard H. Bell (ed.), *Simone Weil's Philosophy of Culture: Readings towards a Divine Humanity* (Cambridge: CUP, 1993), pp. 52–76.

30 COT, p. 6.

31 COT, pp. 6–8.

32 COT, pp. 84.

33 A, p. 242.

34 A, p. 243.

35 TVNL, p. 285.

36 TVNL, p. 184 and 'The philosophical structures of Palamism', p. 41; quoting T. S. Eliot, 'The Dry Salvages' from *Four Quartets*.

37 'The philosophical structures of Palamism', p. 41.

38 TA, p. 144, Williams' italics.

39 OTJ, p. 30.

40 'To stand where Christ stands', in Ralph Waller and Benedicta Ward (eds), *Introduction to Christian Spirituality* (London: SPCK, 1999), pp. 1–13: p. 2.

41 '*Sapientia* and the Trinity: reflections on *De trinitate*', in Bernard Bruning, Mathijs Lamberigts and J. van Houtem (eds), *Collectanea Augustiniana: Mélanges T. J. van Bavel*, vol. 1 (Louvain: Leuven University Press, 1990), pp. 317–32.

42 'The Spirit of the age to come', *Sobornost: The Journal of the Fellowship of St Alban and St Sergius* 6.9 (Summer 1974), pp. 613–26: p. 615.

43 '*Sapientia* and the Trinity', p. 327.

44 '*Sapientia* and the Trinity', pp. 327–8.

45 *OCT*, p. 120, Williams' italics.

46 *OCT*, p. 124.

47 *OCT*, p. 172, my italics.

48 *OCT*, p. 173, Williams' italics.

3 Cloud of Witnesses

1 'On doing theology' (with James Atkinson), in Christina Baxter (ed.), *Stepping Stones: Joint Essays on Anglican Catholic and Evangelical Unity* (London: Hodder & Stoughton, 1987), pp. 1–20: p. 7.

2 'On doing theology', p. 7.

3 'On doing theology', p. 9, my italics.

4 Presidential Address, 12 October 2002 <http://www.churchinwales.org.uk/archbishop/0019e.html>.

5 *OCT*, p. 47; 'Does it make sense to speak of pre-Nicene orthodoxy?' in Rowan Williams (ed.), *The Making of Orthodoxy: Essays in Honour of Henry Chadwick* (Cambridge and New York: CUP, 1989), pp. 1–23: pp. 16–17.

6 *OCT*, p. 55.

7 *OTJ*, p. 159.

8 *OTJ*, p. 160.

9 *DL*, p. 77.

10 *OTJ*, p. 116.

11 *OCT*, pp. 56–7.

12 *DL*, p. 33.

13 'Foreword', in Mark Pryce (ed.), *Literary Companion to the Lectionary: Readings Throughout the Year* (London: SPCK, 2001), p. ix.

14 *OCT*, p. 30.

15 *PTT*, p. 46.

16 'Women and the ministry: a case for theological seriousness', in Monica Furlong (ed.), *Feminine in the Church* (London: SPCK, 1984), pp. 11–27: p. 12.

17 *WK*, p. 2.

18 *WK*, pp. 1–2.

19 *OCT*, p. 33.

20 *OCT*, pp. 31–2.

21 *R*, pp. xiv–xv, Williams' italics.

22 *OTJ*, p. 187, Williams' italics.

23 *OCT*, p. 209, Williams' italics.

24 'Authority and the bishop in the Church', in Mark Santer (ed.), *Their Lord and Ours: Approaches to Authority, Community, and the Unity of the Church* (London: SPCK, 1982), pp. 90–112: p. 97.

25 *OCT*, p. 216.

26 *R*, pp. 102–3.

27 'Foreword', in Henry McAdoo and Kenneth Stevenson, *The Mystery of the Eucharist in the Anglican Tradition* (Norwich: Canterbury Press, 1995), pp. vii–x: p. ix.

28 'Foreword' in *The Mystery of the Eucharist*, p. ix.

29 'Foreword' in *The Mystery of the Eucharist*, p. viii.

30 'Foreword' in *The Mystery of the Eucharist*, pp. viii–ix, Williams' italics.

31 *OCT*, p. 38.

32 'Poetic and religious imagination', *Theology* 80 (May 1977), pp. 178–87.

33 *OCT*, p. 198.

34 *OCT*, p. 199.

35 'What is Catholic orthodoxy?', in Rowan Williams and Kenneth Leech (eds), *Essays Catholic and Radical: A Jubilee Group Symposium for the 150th Anniversary of the Beginning of the Oxford Movement 1833–1983* (London: Bowerdean Press, 1983), pp. 11–25: p. 12.

36 'What is Catholic orthodoxy?', p. 17.

37 'Does it make sense to speak of pre-Nicene orthodoxy?', p. 17.

38 'Teaching the truth', in Jeffrey John (ed.), *Living Tradition: Affirming Catholicism in the Anglican Church* (London: DLT, 1991), pp. 29–43: p. 32.

39 *R*, p. xiii.

40 *COT*, p. 37, Williams' italics.

41 'Teaching the truth', pp. 30–2.

42 *A*, p. 236.

43 'Doctrinal criticism: some questions', in Sarah Coakley and David A. Pailin (eds), *The Making and Remaking of Christian Doctrine: Essays in Honour of Maurice Wiles* (Oxford: Clarendon, 1993), pp. 239–64: pp. 250–1.

44 'Hooker: philosopher, Anglican, contemporary', in Arthur McGrade (ed.) *Richard Hooker and the Construction of Christian Community* (Washington, and Tempe, Ariz.: Centre for Medieval and Renaissance Studies, 1997), pp. 369–83: p. 382.

45 'Newman's *Arians* and the question of method in doctrinal history', in Ian Ker and Alan Hill (eds), *Newman after a Hundred Years* (Oxford: OUP, 1990), pp. 263–85: p. 285.

46 *COT*, p. 37.

47 *OCT*, p. 84.

48 'What is Catholic orthodoxy?', p. 16.

49 'What is Catholic orthodoxy?', p. 18.

50 'Newman's *Arians* and the question of method in doctrinal history', p. 284.

51 'Statements, acts and values: spiritual and material in the school environment', in Stephen Prickett and Patricia Erskine-Hill (eds), *Education! Education! Education! Managerial Ethics and the Law of Unintended Consequences* (Exeter: Imprint Academic, 2002), pp. 167–78: pp. 173–4.

52 *OTJ*, p. 257.

53 *TVNL*, p. 33.

54 Review of Benedicta Ward, *The Wisdom of the Desert Fathers* and *The Sayings of the Desert Fathers*, in *Sobornost: The Journal of the Fellowship of St Alban and St Sergius* 7.3 (Summer 1976), pp. 219–20: p. 219.

55 *OCT*, p. 23.

56 'Newman's *Arians* and the question of method in doctrinal history', p. 283.

57 *A*, pp. 24–5, Williams' italics.

58 'Does it make sense to speak of pre-Nicene orthodoxy?', pp. 11–12.

59 *A*, p. 24.

4   Adulthood and Childhood

1 C. S. Lewis, *The Last Battle*, ch. 12 and ch. 16.

2 Philip Pullman, *The Amber Skyglass*, ch. 38.

3 *OTJ*, p. 186.

4 *R*, p. 80.

5 *WK*, p. 10.

6 *R*, p. 43, emphasis removed.

7 'The theology of personhood: a study of the thought of Christos Yannaras', *Sobornost: The Journal of the Fellowship of St Alban and St Sergius* 6.6 (Winter 1972), pp. 415–30: p. 419.

8 Hildegard Lecture, Thirsk, 7 February 2003 <http://www.archbish opofcanterbury.org/sermons_speeches/>.

9 Hildegard Lecture.

10 'To give and not to count the cost: a sermon preached at Mirfield in February 1976', *Sobornost: The Journal of the Fellowship of St Alban and St Sergius* 7.5 (Summer 1977), pp. 401–3: p. 403.

11 *OTJ*, p. 130.

12 *LI*, p. 153, my italics.

13 *A*, p. 243.

14 *LI*, pp. 99–100.

15 *OTJ*, p. 90.

16 *LI*, p. 104, Williams' italics.

17 *OCT*, pp. 273–4, Williams' italics.

18 *OCT*, p. 269.

19 *OCT*, p. 269, my italics.

20 *OCT*, p. 269.

21 *WK*, p. 144.

22 *OCT*, p. 153.

23 'The suspicion of suspicion: Wittgenstein and Bonhoeffer', in Richard Bell (ed.), *Grammar of the Heart: New Essays in Moral Philosophy and Theology* (San Francisco: Harper & Row, 1988), pp. 36–53: p. 36, Williams' italics.

24 *WK*, ch. 2.

25 *OTJ*, p. 102.

26 *R*, p. 23.

27 'Catholic persons: images of holiness: a dialogue' (with Philip Sheldrake), in Jeffrey John (ed.), *Living the Mystery: Affirming Catholicism and the Future of Anglicanism* (London: DLT, 1994), pp. 76–89: p. 77.

28 *WK*, p. 84.

29 'Christmas Day Meditation', 2002 <http://www.archbishopofcanterbury.org/sermons_speeches/>.

30 'Christmas Message 2002' <http://www.archbishopofcanterbury.org/sermons_speeches/>.

31 'The spirit of the age to come', *Sobornost: The Journal of the Fellowship of St Alban and St Sergius* 6.9 (Summer 1974), pp. 613–26: p. 616, Williams' italics.

32 *R*, pp. 28–9.

33 *R*, p. 30.

34 *TG*, ch. 6.

35 *LI*, p. 112.

36 '"Know thyself": What kind of an injunction?' in Michael McGhee (ed.), *Philosophy, Religion and the Spiritual Life* (Cambridge: CUP, 1992), pp. 211–27: p. 212.

37 'The suspicion of suspicion', p. 44.

38 '"Know thyself"', p. 221.

39 '"Know thyself"', p. 223.

40 *OCT*, pp. 276–89; and *LI*, p. 160.

41 You see, Jesus *does* want me for a sunbeam, to shine for him each day . . .

42 *OTJ*, p. 175, emphasis removed.

43 Review of S. Tugwell, *Ways of Imperfection*, in *New Blackfriars* 67. 799 (November 1986), pp. 501–2: p. 501.

44 *Christianity and the Ideal of Detachment* (Oxford: Clinical Theology Association, 1989), p. 8.

45 *LRW*, p. 8.

46 *WK*, p. 180.

47 'From William Temple to George Herbert: Anglican origins – prayer and holiness' (Melbourne: Institute of Spiritual Studies, 2002), Part 2 <http://www.media.anglican.com.au/news/2002/2002_07/williams_pt2.pdf>, p. 8.

48 'From William Temple to George Herbert: Anglican origins – prayer and holiness' (Melbourne: Institute of Spiritual Studies, 2002), Part 1 <http://www.media.anglican.com.au/news/2002/2002_07/williams_pt1.pdf>, p. 8.

49 *PTT*, p. xvii.

50 'From William Temple to George Herbert', Part 1, p. 9.

51 *TG*, p. 75; cf. *OCT*, p. 76.

52 *COT*, p. 85.

53 *COT*, p. 86.

54 *TG*, pp. 41–2.

55 *COT*, p. 88.

56 '"Religious realism": on not quite agreeing with Don Cupitt', *Modern Theology* 1.1 (October 1984), pp. 3–24: p. 16.

57 *Christianity and the Ideal of Detachment*, p. 11.

58 'Foreword', in Melvyn Matthews, *Rediscovering Holiness: The Search for the Sacred Today* (London: SPCK, 1996), pp. ix–x, Williams' italics.

59 *TG*, p. 33.

60 'The landscape of faith', National Eisteddfod, 8 August 2001 <http://www.churchinwales.org.uk/archbishop/0010e.html>.

61 *LI*, p. 12.

62 *LI*, p. 38, Williams' italics.

63 *LI*, p. 47.

64 'Statements, acts and values: spiritual and material in the school environment', in Stephen Prickett and Patricia Erskine-Hill (eds), *Education! Education! Education! Managerial Ethics and the Law of Unintended Consequences* (Exeter: Imprint Academic, 2002), pp. 167–78: p. 170.

65 'Statements, acts and values', p. 173.

66 'Reaffirming the value of the child' [Sermon following publication of the Waterhouse Report], 24 May 2000 < http://www.churchinwales.org.uk/archbishop/0003.html>.

67 Presidential Address, 10 April 2002 <http://www.churchinwales.org.uk/archbishop/0013e.html>.

68 'Wanted: imaginative, attentive, ideological, inspirational mediators', *Church Times*, 6 October 2000.

5 *Politics and Peace*

1 *TG*, p. 30.
2 *TVNL*, p. 16.
3 *OTJ*, p. 257.
4 *OTJ*, p. 194.
5 Mark Collier and Rowan Williams, *Beginning Now*, Part 1: *Peace-making Theology: A Study Book for Individuals and Groups* (London: Dunamis, 1984), pp. 13–24.
6 *TG*, p. 30.
7 *OCT*, p. 94.
8 'Jesus – God with us' (with Richard Bauckham), in Christina Baxter (ed.), *Stepping Stones: Joint Essays on Anglican Catholic and Evangelical Unity* (London: Hodder & Stoughton, 1987), pp. 21–41: pp. 27–8.
9 'Catholic persons: images of holiness: a dialogue' (with Philip Sheldrake), in Jeffrey John (ed.), *Living the Mystery: Affirming Catholicism and the Future of Anglicanism* (London: DLT, 1994), pp. 76–89: pp. 84–5.
10 Sermon at Canterbury Cathedral, morning service, 2 March 2003 <http://www.archbishopofcanterbury.org/sermons_speeches/>.
11 'The Spirit of the age to come', *Sobornost: The Journal of the Fellowship of St Alban and St Sergius* 6.9 (Summer 1974), pp. 613–26: p. 622.
12 *OTJ*, p. 192.
13 Review of Paul Evdokimov, *L'Esprit Saint dans la tradition Orthodoxe*, in *Sobornost: The Journal of the Fellowship of St Alban and St Sergius* 6.4 (Winter 1972), pp. 284–5: p. 285.
14 'The Spirit of the age to come', p. 621.
15 *R*, ch. 2.
16 *OTJ*, p. 191, Williams' emphasis.
17 *COT*, p. 62, Williams' italics.
18 *OTJ*, p. 148, emphasis removed.
19 'The necessary non-existence of God', in Richard H. Bell (ed.), *Simone Weil's Philosophy of Culture: Readings towards a Divine Humanity* (Cambridge: CUP, 1993), pp. 52–76: p. 66.
20 'The Spirit of the age to come', p. 616; 'The theology of personhood: a study of the thought of Christos Yannaras', *Sobornost: The Journal of the Fellowship of St Alban and St Sergius* 6.6 (Winter 1972), pp. 415–30: p. 419.
21 'Saving time: thoughts on practice, patience and vision', *New Blackfriars* 73.861 (June 1992), pp. 319–26: p. 322.
22 'The Spirit of the age to come', p. 622
23 *OCT*, p. 175.
24 *OCT*, pp. 174–5.
25 'The ethics of SDI', in Richard J. Bauckham and R. John Elford (eds), *The Nuclear Weapons Debate: Theological and Ethical Issues* (London: SCM Press, 1989), pp. 162–74.

26 *OCT*, pp. 101–3.

27 *OCT*, p. 106.

28 *LI*, pp. 58–9.

29 *LI*, p. 70.

30 *OCT*, p. 36.

31 *TG*, p. 66.

32 'Between politics and metaphysics: reflections in the wake of Gillian Rose', *Modern Theology* 11 (January 1995), pp. 3–22: p. 11.

33 *LI*, p. 86.

34 *LI*, p. 114.

35 *LI*, p. 3.

36 *OCT*, pp. 280–3.

37 *LI*, p. 116, my italics.

38 *OCT*, p. 219; cf. 'Christian resources for the renewal of vision', in Alison J. Elliot, Ian Swanson, and Rowan Williams (eds), *The Renewal of Social Vision* (Edinburgh: Centre for Theology and Public Issues, 1989), pp. 2–7: pp. 2–4.

39 'The ethics of SDI', p. 173.

40 'Liberation theology and the Anglican tradition', in David Nicholls and Rowan Williams (eds), *Politics and Theological Identity: Two Anglican Essays* (London: The Jubilee Group, 1984), pp. 7–26: pp. 7–10.

41 The Richard Dimbleby Lecture, broadcast on BBC1, 19 December 2002 <http://www.archbishopofcanterbury.org/sermons_speeches/>.

42 'From William Temple to George Herbert: Anglican origins – prayer and holiness' (Melbourne: Institute of Spiritual Studies, 2002), Part 1 <http://www.media.anglican.com.au/news/2002/2002_07/williams_pt1.pdf>, p. 8.

43 'Being a people: reflections on the concept of the "laity"', in *Reflection on the Laity: A Focus for Christian Dialogue between East and West = Religion, State and Society* 27.1 (1999), pp. 11–18: p. 12.

44 *OCT*, p. 237.

45 'Mankind, nation, state', in Paul Ballard and Huw Jones (eds), *This Land and People: A Symposium on Christian and Welsh National Identity* (Cardiff: Collegiate Centre of Theology, University College, 1979), pp. 119–25.

46 'Barth, war and the state', in Nigel Biggar (ed.), *Reckoning with Barth* (Oxford: Mowbray, 1988), pp. 170–90: pp. 187–8.

47 'Barth, war and the state', pp. 187–8.

48 *Beginning Now*, Part 1: *Peacemaking Theology*, pp. 1–8.

49 *OTJ*, p. 44.

50 *TG*, p. 38.

51 *OTJ*, p. 128.

6 *Sex and the Gospel*

1 'On making moral decisions', in Robin Gill (ed.), *The Cambridge Companion to Christian Ethics* (Cambridge: CUP, 2001), pp. 3–15: p. 6.
2 'On making moral decisions', p. 7.
3 'On making moral decisions', pp. 9–10.
4 'On making moral decisions', pp. 9–10.
5 'On making moral decisions', pp. 9–10.
6 'On making moral Decisions', p. 10.
7 'On making moral decisions', p. 10.
8 'On making moral decisions', p. 11.
9 'The body's grace', in Eugene F. Rogers, Jr (ed.), *Theology and Sexuality: Classic and Contemporary Readings* (Oxford: Blackwell, 2002), pp. 309–21: p. 312.
10 'The body's grace', pp. 312–13.
11 'The body's grace', p. 314
12 'The body's grace', p. 313.
13 'The body's grace', p. 310.
14 'The body's grace', p. 317.
15 *OTJ*, pp. 164–5, emphasis removed.
16 'The body's grace', p. 313.
17 'The body's grace', p. 313.
18 'The body's grace', p. 315.
19 Review of Elizabeth Stuart, *Just Good Friends: Towards a Lesbian and Gay Theology of Relationships,* in *Theology and Sexuality* 4 (March 1996), pp. 123–6: p. 124.
20 'The body's grace', p. 315.
21 Presidential Address, 12 October 2002 <http://www.churchinwales.org.uk/archbishop/0019e.html>.
22 Presidential Address, 27 April 2000 <http://www.churchinwales.org.uk/archbishop/0002e.html>.
23 Presidential Address, 27 April 2000.
24 'The body's grace', pp. 315–16.
25 'The body's grace', p. 320.
26 'Knowing myself in Christ', in Timothy Bradshaw (ed.), *The Way Forward: Christian Voices on Homosexuality and the Church* (London: Hodder & Stoughton, 1997), pp. 12–19: p. 17.
27 'Knowing myself in Christ', p. 14.
28 'Knowing myself in Christ', p. 12.
29 *OCT*, p. 57.
30 'Catholic and Reformed', in *Affirming Catholicism* (Autumn 1993) <http://www.affirmingcatholicism.org.uk/>.
31 A Communiqué from the Primates of the Anglican Communion, 28

March 2000 <http://www.anglicancommunion.org/acns/acnsarchive/acns2075/acns2094.html>.

32 Press Release, 23 July 2002 <http://www.archbishopofcanterbury.org/releases/>.

33 Letter to Primates, 23 July 2002 <http://www.churchinwales.org.uk/archbishop/>.

34 'Authority and the bishop in the Church', in Mark Santer (ed.), *Their Lord and Ours: Approaches to Authority, Community, and the Unity of the Church* (London: SPCK, 1982), pp. 90–112.

Further Reading

General

The last time I printed out my full bibliography of Williams'
writings, it came to thirty-one sides of A4 – and I'm sure I've
missed quite a few, given his tendency to publish in out-of-the-
way corners. The list here, however, is not for those obsessives
like myself who want to read everything, and it is not for those
of academic tendency who want to read his more technical writings, but for those who want a few accessible pointers. In general, I would suggest that someone new to Williams' theology
began with *The Dwelling of the Light* (Norwich: Canterbury
Press, 2003), and *Ponder These Things* (Norwich: Canterbury
Press, 2002) – two short books of meditations on various icons,
which provide a surprisingly complete gateway to the main
themes of Williams' theology – followed by *Silence and Honey-
Cakes* (Oxford: Lion, 2003), some short and very accessible
talks on spirituality. For someone who wanted more, I would
suggest going on to *Open to Judgement* (London: DLT, 2002)
– a collection of Williams' sermons which adds more varied
orchestration, and to his cultural and political discussion in *Lost
Icons* (Edinburgh: T&T Clark, 2000). If you're still going after
that, I'd suggest the meditative exploration of the Gospel stories
in *Resurrection* (London: DLT, 2002) and in *Christ on Trial*
(Grand Rapids: Zondervan, 2002), and then finally the difficult
but rewarding survey of Christian spirituality in *The Wound
of Knowledge* (London: DLT, 2002). For some biographical
background, Rupert Shortt's *Rowan Williams: An Introduction*

(London: DLT, 2003) is very readable – it will also give more hints than I have about some of the sources of Williams' thinking. I would, however, caution strongly against relying on Gary Williams' widely circulated pamphlet *The Theology of Rowan Williams* – its ungenerous conclusions are, in my opinion, upheld by *serious* misunderstandings of Rowan Williams' theology.

Chapter 1: Disarming Acceptance

The main themes of Chapter One can all be found in the sermon Williams gave during his enthronement service (27 February 2003), available on the internet, at <http://www.archbishopof canterbury.org/sermons_speeches>. For more on Jesus, you can look at *The Dwelling of the Light* listed above, and at 'A history of faith in Jesus' – a paper published in Marcus Bockmuehl's *Cambridge Companion to Jesus* (Cambridge: CUP, 2001). If you can get hold of it, one of the best introductions to Williams' understanding of the Incarnation is a chapter he co-wrote with Richard Bauckham in Christina Baxter's *Stepping Stones* (London: Hodder, 1987). At a somewhat more difficult level, you can also try 'Beginning with the Incarnation' in *On Christian Theology* (Oxford: Blackwell, 2000) and 'The seal of orthodoxy' in Martin Warner's *Say Yes to God* (London: Tufton, 2000). I'd also recommend sermons 13, 16 and 32 in *Open to Judgement*.

Chapter 2: The Source of Life

For Chapter Two, both *The Dwelling of the Light* and *Ponder These Things* (listed above) are among the best introductions. You can also look at Williams' chapter, 'To stand where Christ stands' in Ralph Waller and Benedicta Ward's *Introduction to Christian Spirituality* (London: SPCK, 1999), and at sermons 4 and 6 in *Open to Judgement*. At a more difficult level, you can make an attempt on 'Word and spirit', 'Trinity and revelation' and 'On being creatures' in *On Christian Theology*. 'The Nicene heritage', in James M. Byrne (ed.), *Christian Understanding of God Today* (Dublin: Columba, 1993) is not easy to get hold of, but is well worth the search.

Chapter 3: Cloud of Witnesses

For examples of Williams' use of Scripture, see *Christ on Trial* and *Resurrection*, listed above. For Williams' views on the Bible, look also at sermon 28 on the Bible in *Open to Judgement* and at his September 2002 'Presidential Address' to the Church in Wales Governing Body online at <http://www.churchinwales. org.uk/archbishop/> – and, at a harder level, 'The discipline of Scripture' in *On Christian Theology*. If you can find 'The Bible', in I. Hazlett's *Early Christianity: Origins and Evolution to AD 600* (Nashville: Abingdon Press, 1991), it's also worth a look. If you want an example of Williams' attention to the Christian tradition, I'd suggest his *Teresa of Avila* in the Outstanding Christian Thinkers series (London: Geoffrey Chapman, 1991) – his book on *Arius* is fantastic, but very technical. For the Eucharist, try his 1982 Grove booklet on *Eucharistic Sacrifice* (Liturgical Study 31). If you can get hold of it, Williams' article on 'Poetic and religious imagination' in the May 1977 edition of *Theology* (vol. 80) is the best introduction to his views on the growth and use of language. On doctrine, you could try his paper 'Does it make sense to speak of pre-Nicene orthodoxy?' in the book of essays he edited in honour of his teacher Henry Chadwick: *The Making of Orthodoxy* (Cambridge: CUP, 1989) and the paper on 'Doctrinal criticism' in Sarah Coakley and David A. Pailin's *The Making and Remaking of Christian Doctrine* (Oxford: Clarendon, 1993); very clear – but not easy to find – is 'Teaching the truth', in Jeffrey John's *Living Tradition: Affirming Catholicism in the Anglican Church* (London: DLT, 1991).

Chapter 4: Adulthood and Childhood

For Williams' guidance on spirituality, *Silence and Honey-Cakes*, *Resurrection* and *The Wound of Knowledge* (listed above) are among the best guides, but you can also take a look at Williams' 'Hildegard Lecture' (7 February 2003) and his 2002 'Christmas Day Meditation', both online at <http://www.archbishopofcan terbury.org/sermons_speeches>. See also sermons 8, 11, 17, 18 and 22 in *Open to Judgement*, and Williams' booklet *Christianity and the Ideal of Detachment* (Oxford: Clinical Theology Association, 1989). For more on contemplative pragmatism, see 'From William Temple to George Herbert: Anglican Origins – Prayer and Holiness', a series of talks given in May 2002 and published online at <http://www.media.anglican.com.au/ news/2002/2002_07/williams_pt1.pdf> and <http://www.media. anglican.com.au/news/2002/2002_07/ williams_pt2.pdf>. On church schools, see Williams' chapter in Stephen Prickett and Patricia Erskine-Hill's *Education! Education! Education!* (Thorverton: Imprint Academic, 2002) – or the nearly identical paper, 'Room for the Spirit' published online at <http://www.natsoc. org.uk/recentre/lect1999.htm>; see also his April 2002 'Presidential Address' to the Church in Wales Governing Body, online at <http://www.churchinwales.org.uk/archbishop/0013e.html>, and his sermon 'Reaffirming the value of the child', given following publication of the Waterhouse Report in May 2000, and online at <http://www.churchinwales.org.uk/archbishop/0003e. html>.

Chapter 5: Politics and Peace

If you can find it, Williams' 1983 book *The Truce of God* (London: Collins/Fount) is an accessible introduction to what he has to say about peace and community, but you can also look at sermons 23, 26 and 33 in *Open to Judgement*, and at his paper on the Star Wars Defence Initiative online at <http://ccnd. gn.apc.org/RWStarWars.htm>. For more general political and cultural matters, *Lost Icons* (listed above) is the best place to start. If you can get hold of them, his articles on 'Violence and the gospel in South Africa', in *New Blackfriars* 65 (December 1984) and 'Penance in the penitentiary', published in *Theology* 95 (March/April 1992), and his September 2000 Presidential Address to the Church in Wales Governing Body, published online at <http://www.churchinwales.org.uk/archbishop/0005e.html>, are interesting examples of his social and political thinking. *Writing in the Dust* (Grand Rapids: Eerdmans, 2002), his 2001 Christmas message (online at <http://www.churchinwales.org.uk/archbishop/0012e.html>) and his September 2001 Presidential Address to the Church in Wales Governing Body (online at <http://www.churchinwales.org.uk/archbishop/0011e.html>) give Williams' responses to September 11.

Chapter 6: Sex and the Gospel

The best place to start is the difficult but important 'On making moral decisions', a paper delivered at the 1998 Lambeth Conference and published in Robin Gill's *Cambridge Companion to Christian Ethics* (Cambridge: CUP, 2001) or online at <http://www.anglicancommunion.org/acns/lambeth/lc035.html>. On sexual ethics, another difficult but rewarding read is 'The body's grace' (which has been published as a separate pamphlet by the Lesbian and Gay Christian Movement, or as a chapter in Eugene Rogers' *Theology and Sexuality* (Oxford: Blackwell, 2002) or online at <http://www.iconservatives.org.uk/bodys_grace.htm>); see also sermon 29 in *Open to Judgement*, and Williams' April 2000 Presidential Address to the Church in Wales Governing Body (online at <http://www.churchinwales.org.uk/archbishop/0002e.html>). For homosexuality specifically, look at 'Knowing myself in Christ' in Timothy Bradshaw's *The Way Forward* (London: Hodder, 1997). On sharing a Church with those with whom we disagree, see Williams' 1993 paper 'Catholic and Reformed', in *Affirming Catholicism*, available at <http://www.affirmingcatholicism.org.uk/>.

Subject and Name Index